The Modern Day Mother

Babies and Sleep from Womb to One

ANDI LEW

First published in 2012 by Heart to Heart Publishing

Copyright © Andi Lew 2012

All rights reserved. No part of this publication may be reproduced, stored in a retrieval system or transmitted in any form by any means, electronic, mechanical, photocopying, recording or otherwise, without the prior written permission of the publisher and copyright holder.

Andi Lew asserts the moral right to be identified as the author of this work.

National Library of Australia Cataloguing-in-Publication entry:
Author: Lew, Andi
Title: The Modern Day Mother: Babies and Sleep from Womb to 1 / Andi Lew.
ISBN: 978-0-9873504-2-8
ISBN: 978-0-9873504-0-4 (e-Book)
Subjects: Parenting
Dewey Number: 649.1

Address
http://www.andilew.com
www.themoderndaymother.com

DISCLAIMER

All care has been taken in the preparation of the information herein, but no responsibility can be accepted by the publisher or author for any damages resulting from the misinterpretation of this work.

Please note that this book is not intended for the curing or fixing of illnesses.

The Modern Day Mother
Andi Lew

Co-author of health guide *7 Things Your Doctor Forgot to Tell You*, author and mother, Andi Lew, is a certified infant massage instructor, natural nurturer and advocate for healthy living.

Andi Lew was an active member of the Australian Breastfeeding Association. She has appeared on the cover of their magazine and is regular contributor for other magazines such as *Cosmopolitan Pregnancy*, *New Idea*, *Ultra Fit* and *Australian Natural Health*.

She is a TV and radio personality presenting on natural health and parenting, and blogs for model mum Miranda Kerr's KORA organics website.

As an owner and director of her husband's chiropractic wellness centre, Andi is often approached for advice on parenting naturally and where to get support.

www.andilew.com
www.7things.com.au
www.themoderndaymother.com

Acknowledgments

I would like to thank the following authors and publishers for permission to quote from works to which they have rights:

- Dr Bill Sears
- Dr. Sarah J Buckley
- Jo Jackson King

Thank you to Kate Brereton, Janet Murphy, Simone Casey, Martha Sears and Jan Ireland for all your lessons and encouragement. I'd also like to show gratitude to all the family members and friends who gave support, read the manuscript and helped shape this book. Thank you to Vicky Leon for the wonderful photography, including the cover photograph.

Contents

Introduction	1
Foreword	5
Chapter 1: A Perfect Pregnancy	7
Healthier Pregnancy Steps	11
Birth Plans	18
Chapter 2: Bonding at Birth	21
Breathing and Visualisation Techniques	23
Your Birth is Unique	28
Benefits of a Natural Birth	28
After Birth Care	29
Chapter 3: Why is my Baby Waking?	35
Sleep – Rules and Truths	37
Sleep Myths	42
Nurturing Your Baby to Be Self-Reliant	45
Chapter 4: No Cry Babies	47
Your Child has Three Brains	49
Why Babies Don't Cry in Africa	56
Why Babies Don't Cry in the Wild	59
Chapter 5: Breastfeeding Bliss	63
Natural Breastfeeding	63
Benefits of Breastfeeding	67
Understanding Breastfeeding from Baby's Perspective	68
Comparing Human Milk to Animals' Milk	70
Breastfeeding Myths	74
Helpful Hormones	77

Chapter 6: Where's the Village? 81
Getting to Know Your Baby 81
The Village Concept / How to Create a 'Village' 82
Five Easy Things to Help You Cope 88

Chapter 7: Baby Sleep Tips and Myths 91
Natural Sleep Solutions 92
Magic Chiropractic 92
Food Guide 111
Health Benefits of Infant Massage 119
Co-Sleeping: How to Sleep with Your Baby Safely 126

Chapter 8: Empowering You 129
Dealing with Unwanted Criticism 129
Looking After Number Two -- You 132
Separation, Distress and Dealing with it 133
Losing Post Baby Weight 136
Where's the Support? 137

Introduction

Before our first baby, my husband worked as a paramedic in South Africa where he was privy to many births. Often native women wouldn't make it to the hospital and would ask for the vehicle to pull over to the side of the road where they would squat and "get on with it". He shared many stories of how stoic these women are and how natural birth can be with no intervention. He was inspired by how natural it looked and how natural birthing for them is a cultural thing.

When we fell pregnant with our first child, we were inspired by these African women as well as his late grandfather; an obstetrician who loved natural deliveries. As wellness centre owners with a pediatric chiropractic practice, we see the damaging effects intervention can sometimes have during a birthing process, so if it was safe to do so, we were determined to have a natural birth. Luckily we did.

We were blessed with a very wakeful baby. It was viewed as a problem and this left me feeling confused and emotional. Some lactation specialists like bestselling author of *Sleeping Like a Baby* Pinky McKay would call him a 'high interest baby'.

A 'high interest baby' is a great term to describe my baby Beaudy, because he was interested in everything around him and was so aware. I wanted to encourage and nurture that and understand his perception of the world he was taking in on a daily basis. From the time he was born, I knew he knew exactly what was going on around him. He would be sleeping next to his Daddy at two weeks of age, hands behind his head, and I'd lean in to take a picture of them both but Beaudy would open his eyes open at the exact time I took the picture! He stared at the camera and knew what I was doing. You couldn't put anything past him.

In the paediatric chiropractic centre, I see that most other babies know exactly what is going on too. Aren't they just little people? Many mothers would say about their baby, "*Oh he's been here before*", or "*He's an old soul*". These phrases are common because these little people we have made are just that — people. They aren't blobs that we have to train, mould and transform, but rather little souls with their own thoughts,

feelings, emotions and agendas that are valid, real and lovable. Half the fun is getting to know these little people and following their lead so we can try to understand their language and give them what they need and want.

As a new mum I experienced more criticism and judgement than I ever would have thought. Surely, advice was a given and it would come my way; I was prepared for that, but I was not prepared for the extent of it.

The advice, albeit overwhelming, did come from a good place. It was given in a bid to help me get some more sleep. My own mother wasn't able to breastfeed. Her milk "dried up". She was given advice from experts who had little knowledge on breastfeeding and didn't know things have changed and that there is actually good breastfeeding support now. Other mums told me of their sleepless nights and hermit home life. I discovered there is a whole community and world of people looking for ways to help their baby sleep longer or sleep through the night. I also discovered a multi-billion dollar industry producing books and information on controlled crying and letting babies 'cry it out'.

Controlled crying (CC) or cry it out (CIO) methods are being marketed in other ways so mothers don't think it's a cruel method that goes against their instincts. However, a cry is still a cry, no matter what type and how long. It is tempting to go ahead with strict baby training routines when you are feeling tired and desperate, and don't have support. I read about the damaging psychological ramifications for both baby and mother. There had to be another way and other answers.

Telling a baby when to eat, sleep or drink never made sense to me. It would be like someone telling me when to do the same. I found that when my son was placed in my arms, I knew exactly how to listen for his cues and was intuitively responsive, but something kept getting in the way: other people's voices.

Lactation specialist and bestselling author Pinky McKay was one of several positive role models and mentors who educated me about the damaging psychological effects of any type of prolonged crying. Pinky invited me to a teleseminar called the Con of Controlled Crying. Beforehand, I had questions: Ok, it might work, but for how long? Are they really sleeping, or just lying there, given up on hope to call out for you because they've learnt that nobody will come? And in those moments, what are they thinking or feeling and what are the long term effects of training your baby not to ask for you, or learn that the caregiver won't come? When he starts teething or goes through a development phase will I have to retrain him all over again? Why does it break my heart to see him cry?

It breaks my heart to see anyone cry no matter what age. I have a deep empathy for others. It wasn't like babies just cry — End. Of. Story. Babies cry because it's their means of communication and their last, not first, call for help. I learnt we are biologically and hormonally designed to respond to our crying babies. They don't actually need to cry if you listen to their signs and signals.

I've met very few mothers who say they don't have a problem hearing their babies cry. However, most tell me it breaks their hearts and want to find a better way; a gentler way of parenting. I will not judge those mums who choose to do it. You do what you have to do for you and your family. Although, I've observed that women who choose this path quite often lack support. And oh, the places we'd be if we had more of that and less feelings of competition in new mothers' groups.

It's all too common to feel inadequate at child health and maternal nurse routine check-ups and weigh-ins, mothers' groups and even amongst family. The feelings of inadequacy come from weighing, measuring and comparing to 'averages' and other children, instead of celebrating the uniqueness of each child.

With unwanted criticism from family, friends and other mums you wouldn't know how to handle at the best of times, imagine trying to deal with it while you're sleep deprived and hormonal, trying to recover from the experience of birth and get to know your bundle of joy. Who knew that in the most tiring time of your life you would be tested and bombarded with everyone's ideas and opinions about how to raise your child? Couldn't these people wait until you got some sleep or at least give you the space to bond and gain some confidence?

I was tired and confused with the bombardment of information. Most of it was opinions. That is where my search began. I am interested in living 'naturally' so was eager to research natural approaches to parenting. Also, because my husband works with children's nervous systems as a paediatric chiropractor, we were curious to look to see if there was relevant research that could help us with our 'wakeful' baby. It was the research that spoke louder than any words we heard.

My very sleep-deprived journey and the challenges I faced gave me the material and drive to research and write this book. I'm so glad I can now pay it forward. I have been privy to a network of people like Australian Breastfeeding Association counsellors, lactation experts, midwives, Calmbirth® practitioners, chiropractors, doctors, mums, grandmas and authors. They generously shared knowledge that I am compelled to share with you.

This book is for the new mum who is confused and drowning in a sea of others' opinions. The mum who wants to do what her mother did because "it must have worked because I turned out ok", but struggles in her heart because it doesn't feel right. It's for all the mums that pass each other on the street pushing prams wondering if those other mums feel like she does; the mum that hates going to play groups because she doesn't want to have to lie or hear the others talk of their baby 'sleeping through'. It's for the new mamas who had a hard birth or breastfeeding challenges and feel inadequate. It's for all the mothers who cry before putting baby down to sleep feeling anxious because she wonders how long she has to sleep and when her baby will wake next. It's for the mama who has a baby or toddler waking 5-6 times a night so she wonders what she has done 'wrong'. The answer is actually "nothing", especially if you have had your baby checked by a doctor and chiropractor and you have ruled out pathology or vertebral subluxation. Your baby and you are just right.

This mother was me. You may feel relieved to know there are answers that not only make sense, but will help you feel supported in following your heart. You are not alone. There's a whole world of mothers out there connecting and supporting each other online.

You'll feel relieved and empowered. You'll be able to reclaim your inner maternal instincts from this book. You need to be mothered a little after birth so you feel like you can do some mothering. You'll get some great tips and find peace— like we did— when some of the myths surrounding babies and sleep are dispelled.

Every baby is unique. We need to approach parenting techniques with this in mind — gently, making them work for your modern day family and doing what's right for you.

As long as you have the research, science and facts about your baby's brain and how it works, you'll be able to parent naturally, make an informed choice and hopefully feel a little less isolated along the way.

We are excited to share with you our story and some amazing research that will help you make sense of it all and hopefully get some 'golden' sleep!

Foreword

Having a baby is an amazing experience – from giving birth to meeting your beautiful newborn and watching this new person unfold into a delightful, unique little being. However, if you don't yet have a baby, most mothers would agree that the road ahead should be signposted with warnings that your journey could be 'bumpy' or even 'rocky'.

Babies are the ultimate 'connectors' – they bring family, friends and even complete strangers together. Everyone loves to share the magic of a newborn! They also like to share advice, and here lies the problem: this mountain of advice can be overwhelming to a new mother. Every new mother wants to do the best by her baby but it seems everyone she talks to and every book she picks up is claiming there is one right way to care for this precious little bundle – but the 'right' way depends on who is sharing advice.

It is very difficult to think logically when you are vulnerable and sleep deprived and your brain is bathed in a cocktail of new mummy hormones that make you feel as protective as a mother lioness towards your little one. This is why advice that may sound completely logical at one level can do your head in because often what sounds 'rational' is competing with what feels intuitive and, when you are a new mother, you are primed to operate on intuition. This is so commonly accepted that it even has labels – the 'motherhood mindset' or 'maternal pre-occupation'.

When a baby cries, if this is YOUR baby, you not only 'hear' your baby crying, but you 'feel' your baby's cries piercing deeply within your body. You and your baby are chemically, hormonally wired to be close to each other: your baby communicates in the only way available to him and you are hard wired to respond. In Stone Age days, this would have ensured your baby's survival. Of course, there are no longer sabre toothed tigers prowling about but your baby doesn't know this, nor does he know he is in a safety standards approved cot with a video monitor on the wall so you can observe his every breath. To your baby, being separated from you is stressful – you may as well be in another country as just in the next room.

Is it any wonder you feel out of your depth some days as you struggle between your intuitive urges to be close to your baby and meet his needs, and trying to make sense of popular advice and the dire warnings that come with most of it? You are sure to hear that you will 'make a rod for your back' if you respond to every cry, as your body is aching to pick up your unsettled baby and comfort him, or that your child will not develop 'essential skills' such as learning to put himself to sleep if you don't 'teach him' by leaving him to cry alone. You will no doubt be told that you mustn't allow your baby to fall asleep on the breast (despite hormones in your breast milk that induce relaxation and sleep); that you mustn't rock him to sleep; that he will be clingy or dependent if you let him 'get used to' cuddles or being carried in a sling and, above all, you mustn't let this baby wrap you around his proverbial little finger.

Thankfully, you won't hear any of this confusing advice here. I have had the greatest pleasure watching Andi Lew grow from the confusion and self-doubt of new motherhood to an empowered, confident mother who wants to 'pay it forward' by sharing her personal journey in this book. Andi stayed strong along the bumpy road of undermining advice and social pressures as she followed her intuition to nurture her son Beaudy naturally and respectfully. She also took on the responsibility of doing her own research along the way – she discovered that there was a plethora of evidence to validate her choices and she is sharing that with you too. As well as being armed with the evidence, Andi has proof in the 'pudding' that her choices are the best ones for her child — her beautiful son, Beaudy!

Although there is a range of choices to suit each unique parent and child, when we meet the needs of babies and nurture with respect, our connection with this wondrous little person will grow strong. Then, even on 'bumpy days' we will be able to trust ourselves and this powerful connection and we will know what to do or where to look for support to smooth the way for our child and ourselves, and we will nurture with confidence.

Pinky McKay, International Board certified Lactation Consultant (IBCLC), runs a private practice in Melbourne, Australia, specialising in gentle parenting techniques. A sought after keynote speaker and best-selling author with four titles published by Penguin, including her recent book Parenting By Heart, *she's an expert source for media, appearing regularly on major network TV and quoted in various publications. Pinky's books, parenting resources and her free newsletter* Gentle Beginnings *can be found on her website:* **www.pinkymckay.com.au**

Chapter One

A Perfect Pregnancy

"Attending births is like growing roses. You have to marvel at the ones that just open up and bloom at the first kiss of the sun but you wouldn't dream of pulling open the petals of the tightly closed buds and forcing them to blossom to your time line."

— Gloria Lemay

May I congratulate you on your journey on wanting to be the best mama for your baby and let you know that you *are* enough for your darling child? You are the perfect parent for your baby. In fact, your baby already chose you as its parent, has decided he wants to learn from the mistakes you are going to make, and wants to learn and grow from them. So you can relax knowing that you can't go wrong. Your loving intent is enough.

Finding out you are pregnant can bring up myriad emotions — excitement, shock, nervousness, elation, self-doubt, and the list goes on. From the day I saw those two stripes on the 'pee' stick; my whole life flashed before me faster than my mother-in-law could plan her next trip to Australia to visit her new grandchild!

My new life with this 'other person' I was about to meet, had begun. My husband Warren, a pediatric chiropractor, was equally thrilled as he has a 'calling' to care for kids. In fact, many mums call him the baby whisperer. However as first time parents-to-be, we were still oh so naïve as to what was about to come. I later learned this was a good thing as you go with your natural instinct to nurture and listen to your babies cues on how to parent or birth.

When we think the best kind of health, we think of 'organic' and terms like 'wellness' and 'prevention'. The term organic is widely used now and it seems like

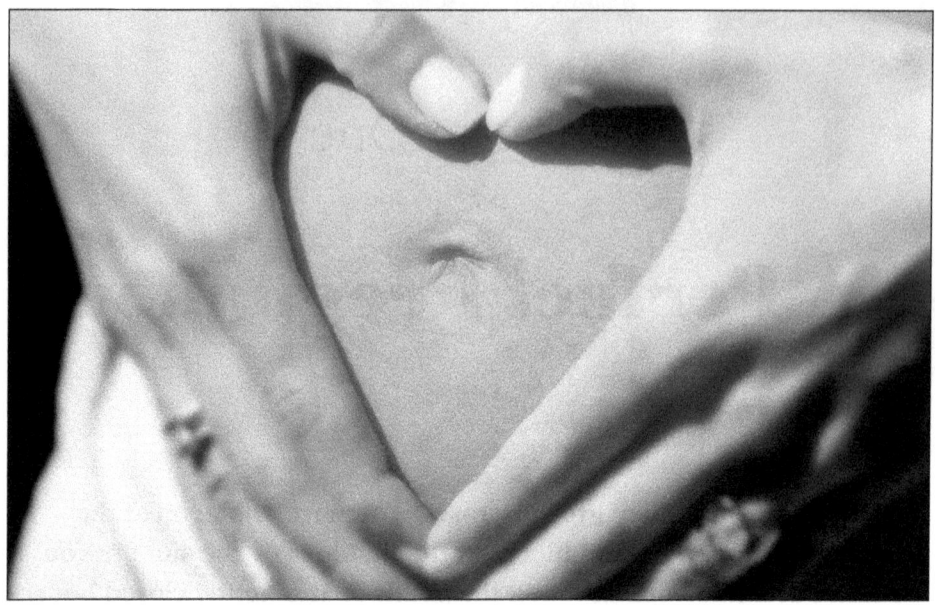

everyone wants organic food or to be living an organic lifestyle. There are organic personal hygiene products, and bio-dynamic produce where health conscious people can take it one step further and make sure the food has been farmed in organic soil that wasn't contaminated with pesticides. In our grandparents' days everything was organic because we didn't have our foods sprayed like we do now, so the term didn't even exist. Organic actually means 'natural'. Yet at this time of a booming wellness revolution, with everyone striving for better health, companies are cashing in on the overused word. When I planned to have our baby, I wanted to continue my organic lifestyle and do what came naturally, or at least what was natural to do.

It's important to be realistic about the full range of emotions women can feel during pregnancy and how they differ throughout each stage too. These are not only normal, evolutionary emotions, but we are blue-printed that way, so they're natural too.

Normal labour is defined as spontaneous onset of labour with a foetus head presentation, where the head is pointing towards the vagina after 37 weeks of pregnancy. The amniotic fluid is clear, the fetal heart rate is within 120-160 beats per minute and the cervix dilates at 1cm or more every hour with progressive descent of the head. The foetus can be birthed up to 10 days after the estimated due date of 40 weeks. However, keep in mind that conception involves a lot of guesswork too. How do we really know when we conceived or even when the sperm met the egg? It may have taken 3 days. A healthy pregnancy and labour takes all of this into consideration.

During the first trimester of pregnancy (the first 3 months), quite often your stomach won't be showing at all. Some have said they didn't even know they were pregnant. When you first find out, it's normal for a new mother to go through a grieving process as she starts to understand or reflect that she will have a very different life. Perhaps this may include having to give up her career she loves, at least for a period of time? Her soon-to-be new role as a mother may feel daunting and some women question whether they'll be adequate in this new important role, or miss the life they had before. The transition is a big one: from an independent woman to a devoted mother with a dependant who will rely on her 24-7. The western world woman has strong feelings because of the dramatic transition in roles. Be assured that it's very healthy and normal to feel this way. Just like with any transition, it's just that: a transition. It takes 9 months to create the baby and as you slowly adapt, you get used to the new thoughts and emotions.

Your body is changing rapidly and so are the hormones. . You may not look pregnant yet and you may have decided not to tell anyone the news so it's understandable to feel all of these things. Some women have doubts about themselves as a mother or worry whether their baby will be okay. You may also feel nauseous or more tired and experience other physical signs and manifestations as you slowly learn and adjust. You will be able to change your perception so these 'symptoms' serve you, encouraging you to take time to rest, relax, nurture yourself and slow down. It's the time to reflect or plan and prepare for a role and chapter ahead that is both life-enhancing and affirming.

I remember having anxiety about how I could possibly be the best mother for this perfect child? My naturopath helped me with some tincture but also did some Reiki healing on me that brought up feelings I didn't really realise I had. She told me something very calming. She said: "Your baby has chosen you as its mother remember? The mistakes you may make — your baby wants to learn from." It helped me to know that I may not be perfect, but I was going to be the perfect mother for my child.

As you ease into the second trimester of pregnancy, not only will you feel a little better but you will start to physically relax more as a hormone called oxytocin kicks in. This hormone makes you feel tired, but evolution has given you this hormone so that you can relax, rest and read and prepare for the marathon that lies ahead. The other hormone that comes to visit you is relaxin, which helps to loosen muscles and ligaments in your pelvis, loosening you up for birthing. You will start to feel kicking and this will help you to bond with your baby as it starts to feel real. You may also look pregnant, so people may give up their seat for you!

Bonding here is paramount for a healthier birth. Oxytocin is the hormone of love which helps you to bond with your baby especially in the last trimester, helping you to get into a primal and loving state that allows you to birth easier. During this time, it's great to read up about birthing and parenting and surround yourself with support groups such as the Australian Breastfeeding Association, as it's never too early to learn about it if this is what you choose to do. (Your baby's birth may take you by surprise or you may need to rest more depending on how it went so there may not be time to start researching once baby is born.) During this time it's important to take lots of baths. Get your partner or if you're doing this on your own, get a friend to massage you and then schedule extra sleep. This is also a pretty good time to get together with a Calmbirth® practitioner and start meditations so you can visualise and plan your ideal birth. It's important to have a birth plan, detailing your birth preferences and wishes, which we will cover a little later in the book.

As health professionals and natural lifestyle advocates, Warren and I are used to being in tune with our bodies and using symptoms as a sign for wellness. We address the cause not just the symptom with our chiropractic lifestyle. We took the same approach to make sure we had a healthy pregnancy.

Your sense of smell will become really strong and this is your body's natural way of telling you to avoid things that are reactive and that your baby doesn't want. It is believed that the mother goes off certain foods so she eats foods the baby will want to get a taste for through her milk once it is born. The diet becomes similar and familiar. They may also be non-reactive foods that are more easily digestible for their developing digestive system. A list of foods to avoid can be obtained from your doctor, naturopath and lactation specialist. The main thing to remember is that the baby gets exactly what you get, so avoiding alcohol and caffeine is paramount. So too is removing large amounts of sugar and salt from your diet to avoid pathological complications such as gestational diabetes or pre-eclampsia. Being healthy and avoiding all these sorts of stimulants allows you to be more in tune with your body. You may find that you are naturally turned off these things anyway and crave foods your body needs, like dark leafy greens when you are low in iron, for example.

During this stage, it's also important to make peace with whatever birth you may have, however it may unfold. After all, it's your birth and nobody else's. Each experience is so unique like each person born. Every baby's birth journey is as unique as them.

It's during the 3rd trimester that you will really need to listen to your body and take it slower. High blood pressure resulting in a condition called pre-eclampsia is a leading cause of death for mother and baby during this stage of pregnancy. Your check-ups with your midwife or obstetrician will make sure you are okay, but it's best to avoid anything that may increase your blood pressure.

At this stage, you may like to talk to your midwife or doctor about what may happen if intervention occurs and what you would like to happen. Any stage of your pregnancy is a great time to discuss your fears and concerns with your partner, or support person, Calmbirth® practitioner or midwife. If you want a natural birth, be at peace with the fact that even though you will do everything you can to facilitate that, it might not happen. You and your team will do whatever they can to ensure it goes according to your birth plan, so all you need to know is that you tried your best and your birth experience will be yours.

Midwives and Mothers Australia (MAMA) is an organisation that can support you. The organisation's belief is that pregnancy, labour and birth are profound events. They respect mothers as active participants in decisions regarding their pregnancy, birth and wellbeing. They will provide guidance based on each mum's unique circumstances to achieve the best outcome for mother and baby, and provide additional support to families who have chosen other primary models of pregnancy care, be it obstetrics, general practice or allied health professions.

Another MAMA aim is to provide affordable private midwifery care throughout pregnancy, birth and early parenting, in order to enhance women's and families' health during this wonderful but challenging time. MAMA aims to focus on services that are under-resourced in the community, such as the provision of early postnatal care. It's nice to know you are never alone.

Healthier Pregnancy Steps

Morning Wellness

We've all heard of the term morning sickness. In fact, it is the most common thing women say they don't look forward to with pregnancy. They sometimes complain more about this than the birthing process itself! For some it can be a very challenging time. But what if the reason you have morning sickness is because you are actually well? What if it's because your hormones are really strong and working well? Let's call it morning wellness now, and as well as changing our perception of what it is, discover how we can minimise symptoms.

Consider it a 'cleanse and eat clean phase'. Some research has suggested that the act of vomiting while pregnant is actually a way of bringing up something you have ingested that your baby doesn't like, in order to protect the baby. During my first trimester, I only ate fresh food and hardly any packaged food containing preservatives. My body was telling me that this new human growing inside of me wanted only high-quality nutrition. Eating simple, clean and even organic foods ensured I was giving the growing baby excellent nutrition and nothing too complicated for its delicate and developing nervous system.

When the healthy hormones kick in, you may not feel like eating much at first, as I did. Opening the fridge can be the last thing you want to do, especially when your sense of smell heightens and you are turned off strong-smelling foods. When you feel nauseous when you are not pregnant, you choose not to eat, but having a baby means you can't afford to do that. So I soon learnt that forcing myself to eat very small amounts regularly would mean my body wasn't producing too much bile from having an empty stomach. Lack of food can lead to the overproduction of bile in your gut and this may make you feel nauseous; so find something you can handle and make sure it's in reach first thing in the morning. Your stomach has usually been empty for at least 6-8 hours and you want to make sure you keep it full so the bile production doesn't occur.

What you shouldn't eat and avoid while you are pregnant is just as important as what you should eat.

During the first trimester, folate is needed for the health of the baby. Folate is found in avocados but you can also get a supplement with folate and a mix of essential B vitamins. Iron is another essential mineral. Iron is vital as it's required in almost double the usual quantity due to the increase in your blood volumes. Drinks that contain caffeine also inhibit the absorption of iron; yet another reason to avoid coffee and soft-drinks.

Another possible reason for morning wellness may be the consumption of artificial foods. Packaged items containing artificial sweeteners may cause your body to become more sensitive in order to protect your growing foetus. Consuming something so unnatural, experts suggest, may even potentially harm your developing foetus. (Aspartame Toxicity Info Center)

Artificial sweetener may be found in chewing gums, light yogurts and many other packaged foods like diet soft drinks that have "no sugar" or "sugar free" on the label. Some consume them because they believe an artificial sweetener is actually healthier and better for them than sugar. It is not — all artificial sweeteners are exactly that: artificial.

You may have thought it would help you to control your weight. You will gain an average of around 10-14 kg in a healthy pregnancy.

Do artificial sweeteners help us fight the battle of the bulge? A recent study by American GP Dr Joseph Mercola suggests not. There are no studies proving diet drinks assist weight loss.

Remember your uterus is a muscle too, so it will benefit from the magnesium. Keep it functioning well as it houses your baby; it will need to contract optimally when it is finally ready to open up and let your beautiful bundle out into the world!

Also, know that no matter how much you try to have a great diet and relax, you may be suffering from hormone imbalance that existed pre-pregnancy, causing you to feel debilitatingly nauseous no matter what you do. It's important to try and be as healthy as possible prior to conceiving and manage this carefully.

Cravings As Clues

Sometimes pregnancy cravings are actually clues for what your body needs. If you are craving sweet, sugary foods, this usually means you are lacking magnesium. Those who crave icy poles or ice cubes need more iron in their diet. Many women can be depleted of iron during pregnancy, so it's a good idea to get your iron levels checked. Allowing yourself to have a special unhealthy 'treat' once or twice a day may be fine, but if sugar cravings become a regular occurrence you may like to reassess your food intake and make sure you and your baby are getting the best nutrition possible. You may also need more sleep or protein and find you're instead going to sugar for a quick fix.

Skin And Teeth

Your skin may be drier or oilier than usual. While some women experience breakouts in the first trimester; these will settle down. Your skin's colour may change due to extra melanin levels in your skin during pregnancy, so you may find that just a little time in the sun makes you very tanned. It's important to not only avoid the harsh sun and sunburn as you normally would, but to only use a sunscreen cream that doesn't have any nasty chemicals. There are many good organic, paraben-free sunscreens on the market now that you can find in a health or health food shop. What you put on your skin soaks in through the pores. Your skin is a carrier, not a barrier, so make sure you choose only the most natural ingredients when using any personal care products.

Around 75% of women will naturally get stretchmarks, but these can be avoided with a healthy diet and by applying a good oil. Vitamin E, Rose hip oil and cold-pressed organic coconut oil are all good oils to use on your baby bump and of course the rest of your body too. Stretch marks eventually fade once your baby is born.

Dental care is equally as important during pregnancy because high progesterone levels make the margins of the gums around teeth soft and this predisposes them to infection. So make sure you not only brush, but also floss regularly, especially since your appetite will increase and you may find you eat more frequently. If that is the case, you will need to brush more often. It is also important to have regular check-ups and hygiene cleans.

Schedule Sleep

Sleep is underrated, especially during pregnancy. The most important thing you can do for your body while you are pregnant is sleep. Cells replenish when you sleep. Your baby gets to move more and become more active when you sleep, and this actually helps its brain to develop and grow. You resting means your baby gets smarter. Sleep has been shown to decrease food cravings, increase your feel-good chemical levels and endorphins and make you less moody, which can be very good for your partner. Remember that you have a person breathing, feeding, growing and even hanging off you, so all of this requires extra energy and means you need more rest than usual. Listen to your body and schedule in a daily nap.

Don't Stop Exercising

The amount of exercise you do during pregnancy will depend largely on your degree of fitness for the months and years before pregnancy. The fitter you are entering this body-changing time, the better.

Luckily for you, you're already doing everything you can. Clinical studies show that exercise is significant to the mother and child. By circulating blood around the body, more oxygenation is achieved and waste products are removed more efficiently. This is important because the baby also uses the mum's detoxification and excretory system so the quicker it gets out, the better for mum.

Pregnancy is a marathon rather than a sprint, which is why it necessitates a 9-month gestation, so treat your exercise during this time in the same way. For the first trimester (12 weeks), your exercise routine will not have to alter much (unless you are experiencing significant morning wellness). Only as the spine changes to accommodate the growing baby will you have to modify how you train, focusing on your posture to ensure you are exercising the right muscles.

There are three curves in your spine, when looking at it from the side, which are accentuated as the pregnancy progresses. This places extra weight on the joints of your spine, related ligaments and muscles. Exercising should definitely include core stabilisation sets to provide support for the changing physiology. Using a fitness ball is excellent for this. When doing lunges and squats, place the fitness ball in the small of your back and lean with it against a wall for support.

Women have become fearful about hard exercise during pregnancy. This should not be the case as there are women who do triathlons early into the 3rd trimester. The degree of fitness leading up to the pregnancy will be a guide for what you can do during pregnancy. If you're really concerned, you may like to wear a heart rate monitor, but

I found if I just listened to my body, it would tell me to stop when I was training too hard. You may become breathless or feel faint. These are signs that the muscles are taking more blood and giving less to the baby. You may get these signs to tell you to stop or at least slow down. Listen to them.

Things like squats, dead lifts and overhead presses should be modified because of the increase in lumbar lordosis. Modification may mean a lighter weight, a seated rather than standing posture and, most importantly, a detailed and vigilant focus on posture.

To ensure you have correct posture when training, look straight forward, focus on drawing your navel toward your spine, slightly contract your buttocks, and imagine there is a ball in between your shoulder blades and you have to keep it there and prevent it from falling.

Look After Your Lifeline

Your spine is the lifeline that houses your delicate nervous system, which controls and co-ordinates every cell, tissue and organ in your body. Keeping your spine aligned and moving well is imperative for a healthy pregnancy. It oxygenates your body and provides healthy signals from your brain to every part of your body. Research posted by The International Chiropractic Pediatric Association showed that 84% of women receiving chiropractic care during pregnancy reported relief of back pain during pregnancy. There was also significantly less likelihood of back pain during labour, and the women studied had shorter and easier labours and less need for pain medication during birth[1].

My husband, Melbourne chiropractor Dr. Warren Sipser, says: "As your body changes shape with the increased load of being pregnant, your joints have to work harder. You also release hormones such as relaxin, which softens joints even more. This may become a problem if your spine or pelvis is already misaligned as it can compromise the normal movement. Things like back pain and pelvic instability are not normal occurrences during pregnancy. Having chiropractic check adjustments may make your pregnancy and birth so much easier and healthier for you and your baby."

Schedule an appointment with your local wellness chiropractor who is trained to detect and correct vertebral subluxations (spinal misalignment and nervous system interference).

---

[1] Fallon J DC. Proceedings of the World Chiropractic Congress: 1991 (pg. 24-31)

Go To Your Naturopath

It's great to get your iron and folate levels checked. The mother is the last to receive as your baby's needs are more important. Naturopaths can be good for giving you all sorts of natural remedies for morning sickness, sleeplessness or general fatigue that won't harm your baby. Choose a naturopath that uses an objective measure of health like iridology (looking at your health through your eyes/iris), or a live blood cell analysis. That way, you aren't only relying on symptoms to check your health.

Employ A Calmbirth® Practitioner

We wanted to find a Calmbirth® practitioner who we resonated with. It took us a couple of times to find the right one. We found a really nice local woman who is a registered Calmbirth® practitioner. The meditations and breathing techniques really helped us to relax once a week for a few weeks while we focused on our 'calm' birth. Even if the partner falls asleep in the process, they are being programmed on a subconscious level and it's a nice bonding rest anyway. We would fall asleep listening to the meditations at night. I wasn't 100% 'calm' during Beaudy's birth, but I was calm the majority of the time. I was able to allow the other hormones like oxytocin kick in to make me feel relaxed and let my cervix thin and open. I used up less energy during my first stage of labour so that by the time the second stage kicked in, I had conserved some energy to be able to continue.

A Private Midwife?

Initially, we weren't sure what kind of birth we wanted. A lifelong obstetrician, Warren's grandfather may have been a staunch proponent of natural birthing, but he pointed out to us that times had changed and intervention was more common.

We decided our plan of action would be to lessen the chances of intervention so we could avoid it unless completely necessary. We thought that if we had a private midwife that was as experienced in birth as Warren's grandfather, she could coach us and help us get back into the 'zone' or think of other things that may work for us, in order to maximise the chances of a natural birth. Most of the time your obstetrician will only arrive towards the end of the birth anyway.

Our midwife only practised home births. We decided against a home birth because we wanted to have the option of intervention should it be required, but knew we didn't want a hospital birth either. The 'Modern Day Mother' middle ground of doing things naturally, but being careful too, meant we opted for something in between and found a birthing centre that was part of the public system and attached to the hospital. This gave us the peace of mind we needed. All hospitals have midwives there to help you through your birth. But the bonus of having a private midwife was that she learned about us and what made mum tick. So that when it came to show time, she knew which strings to pull and which buttons to push. Our midwife was also available from 3am, which was when the contractions started to get strong. She made it a really beautiful and enjoyable experience, dancing around our bedroom with us to our favourite music while I ate my favourite bowl of mango and sheep's milk yoghurt. We talked about that day being my baby's 'birth day' and we celebrated it right then and there. It made dilating easier and she was on call from word go. She then travelled with us to the birth centre and joined the other midwives. I had a team of dedicated and loving women to help me feel comfortable.

Private health care may not pay for this, but the cost in comparison to the doctor's bills is so minimal that it's really worth considering if it helps you feel more relaxed or have more peace of mind.

Hiring a private midwife or has been known to result in:
- 50% reduction of caesarean rate
- 25% shorter labour
- 60% reduction in epidural requests
- 30% reduction in analgesia use
- 40% reduction in forceps delivery

Hire A Tens Machine

You can get one of these from www.tensaustralia.com.

TENS is an acronym for Transcutaneous Electrical Nerve Stimulation. It is a safe, non-invasive, drug-free option perfect for doing things naturally. The tiny impulses the TENS machine creates along the spine don't take the pain away but they do provide a distraction during each contraction that allows you to focus on other things and be distracted from the area. This was my lifesaver. I was so focused on my breathing as a result. It was like an itch that needed to be scratched with each contraction and the TENS did the scratching!

Other benefits of the TENS are:
- Small and portable
- Increased feeling of wellbeing
- Cost-effective
- Natural option for pain management
- Increased autonomy and independence
- May give your birth partner a job to feel like part of the support team by pressing the button for you every contraction
- You may be entitled to claim from your health insurance provider
- If necessary, it can be applied at the same time as other treatments.

Create Your Birth Wishes

If you consider what's natural or gentle when putting together your birth plan, you'll be able to make active choices for you and your baby that will help your baby have an easier transition into the world. Putting yourself in their shoes from day one is a great way to ensure a special bond and a happy baby.

If you are planning to have a natural birth then it's important to know that despite the very best of intentions things may not end up the way you planned. If you have a birth plan, you are at least making sure that there is a greater likelihood of a natural birth. It is also important to know what will happen if intervention is necessary, so you are prepared.

When writing your birth wishes, please consider those who are going to be your help and support. Write a few words of gratitude, thanking them to take the time to read through your birth plan and for trying to help you as much as possible to achieve your dream birth.

Is there special music you would like to labour and give birth to? It can be slow and without lyrics (relaxation music) or a favourite song that's quite upbeat and rhythmic for you to dance and get active to. After all, you are celebrating a birth day and besides, labour can be very long. It's fun to mix up styles of music depending on what stage of labour you are in, to help you stay focused. If you are musical, you may like to have your partner play the guitar or you may like to sing a song. Singing is a wonderful way to focus on breathing.

I have included our birth plan here to help you get thinking about what you would like. Your signatures are most important, so don't forget to date and sign it before handing it over to your team.

Our Birth Plan

Thank you for taking the time to read this. We appreciate your efforts in helping us create our ultimate birth.

Support Team:
- *Jane Ireland – midwife (contact phone number)*
- *Dr Warren Sipser – husband (contact phone number)*
- *Andrea (Andi) Lew – mother to be (contact phone number)*
- *During labour we plan to use skills we have learned from Calmbirth classes and from Jan Ireland.*
- *Please do not suggest the use of medication. We are aware that it is available and prefer that you assist Andi's support team to refocus; get back into the 'zone'. Please change the environment continually by dimming lighting, changing positions, chiropractic adjustments by Warren, massage, TENS machine, baths, use of water, positive and encouraging phrases and holding the baby's clothing, music.*
- *We are only open to medication in the case of an emergency; if it is a matter of a health and or life concern for the mother and baby. Rest assured that you have our full cooperation if this is the case.*
- *We prefer minimal monitoring of the foetal heart beat.*
- *We prefer not to have internal vaginal examinations unless they are medically necessary.*
- *We prefer that the waters break only naturally and if in the case of an emergency they need to be ruptured, we require you to discuss this with us first.*
- *We prefer no induction unless there is a medical emergency; so discuss with us.*
- *Please discuss with us what intervention may be required and involve us in all decisions.*
- *We prefer to that Andi tears naturally, as opposed to having an episiotomy.*
- *We request that our baby be given immediate skin to skin contact by either Jan, Warren and then of course Andi, and please then place the baby on Andi's chest.*
- *The cord is only to be clamped once the pulsation has ceased and to be cut by Warren.*
- *We prefer no Vitamin K so please discuss with us first. We do not want Hepatitis B vaccination under any circumstances and to be discussed only after birth.*
- *We would prefer to bath our baby the next day after it is born.*
  Parents' signatures

  ....

The main things to decide when writing your birth wishes:

- Who are your birth companions?
- How active would you like to be?
- Prepare or discuss delivery positions
- What kind of natural things would you like to do for labour contractions? For example, Calmbirth® techniques, chiropractic, massage, touch, water pressure or bath, TENS machine, etc.
- In a case of emergency like a caesarean section delivery, you may be under a general anaesthetic and they may decide to only give your baby to you after a period of time. You can actually request for your baby to be put on you straight after birth, even though it is standard procedure to take the baby away. You can also request for your baby to be handed to your husband immediately after the birth.
- What will you do with the umbilical cord? It is common practice to cut the cord pretty soon after birth. However, you may decide to write in your birth plan that you would like the cord to only be cut once the cord has stopped pulsating. Some medical doctors say that the cord has a pulse in it right up until mother and baby have decided they are ready to detach. This is called a Lotus birth; the cord is allowed to remain intact with the placenta still attached until the cord dries and falls off naturally. (More on this later.)

Chapter Two

Bonding at Birth

"Giving birth should be your greatest achievement not your greatest fear."

— Jane Weideman

Bonding between the Western world woman and her baby may not always come naturally as so many factors can get in the way. How does a 'modern day mother' get to experience an empowered birth in an overtly litigious interventionist society?

Carla Hartley, founder of Trust Birth and the Ancient Art Midwifery Institute, says: "We've put birth in the same category with illness and disease and it's never belonged here. Birth is naturally safe, but we've allowed it to be taken over by the medical community."

Some of the fear an expectant mother may feel may come from her perception of birthing. It may get in the way of enjoying the pregnancy. However, you can work at the bond with your child at conception or when you first find out the wonderful news.

Bonding at pregnancy and especially at birth can set up foundations for an easier breastfeeding journey and entry into your new family life. The bond that is created at birth can set up a foundation of wonderful attached parenting and a new love, admiration and respect for you and your partner. While he is in awe of her strength, she is in awe of his support.

We were fortunate to have a natural vaginal birth without drugs or intervention. There are many cases of babies turning in the last weeks or even minutes to become breached. It is not uncommon for women to have a vaginal breach birth. It can happen. No matter what birth you have, or how it leaves you feeling, you can create a special bond. The bonding that occurs through adversity is huge too. The main thing is you recognise the importance of birth, no matter what type, for the purpose of bonding. You are all a team on the birth day and even greater: you are now a family!

You can increase your chances of having baby present well. For example, acupuncture has been known to help lessen labour pain and help with presentation. There's even a chiropractic technique called the Webster technique that can help a baby to turn if it is in a breach position. It is safe, effective and scientific. There are over 100 chiropractic techniques. Making sure the pelvis is in correct alignment allows for more room in the womb for the baby to present better.. You also allow your body to function, without nerve system interference, to its full potential by taking pressure off the nervous system with gentle, specific chiropractic adjustments. The bonus is that not only are you receiving the care but your baby is too.

Having a natural birth is healthier for the baby. There are two types of 'natural' births. There's a vaginal birth — a true natural birth is a vaginal birth without drugs or episiotomy (a cut in the perineum near the anus). The benefits of not having drugs mean the baby doesn't receive anything either.

To increase your chances of a natural birth, you may also like to start with perineal massage. The perineum is the area of the body between the vagina and the anus. Since the 1980s, there has been increased interest in using perineal massage to help minimise or prevent tearing. At present, the research indicates that women having their first baby can lessen their chances of requiring stitches if they do regular perineal massage in the last few weeks of pregnancy, but that it will not necessarily prevent tearing. Your partner can also perform the massage. For every 13 women who may tear but do perineal massage, one woman will avoid stitches.

Allowing yourself to tear naturally if a tear is to happen, is never really felt during the time of labour. It may feel a little sore afterwards, but the oxytocin and love you get from your bundle of joy is what truly helps you forget about any pain. Your body really does have and produce all the chemicals and natural drugs it needs to get you through this. Tearing naturally means you can heal quicker too. Mother gets to recover quicker because a natural tearing allows the skin to tear in a zig-zag shape. A cut from a doctor happens in a straight line, but skin bonds better in a cross patterned/zig-zag fashion. When the doctor cuts you, it's called an episiotomy. It is harder to heal and for skin to bond with a cut like this and stitches may be necessary. Although, stitches are now dissolvable so you may not need them removed. Manuka honey applied to that area has also been known to help fast track healing. Whatever happens during the birth, it's special for you and, at the end of the day, it's your personal and unique experience.

I had a friend who tried so hard to make sure this happened and in the end had to have an emergency c-section. She felt disappointed as she had done Calmbirth® classes. Her son's malpresentation meant it just wasn't possible. But I reassured her that she had no need to be disappointed. After all, she still got to relax through the journey of her last trimester of pregnancy, so it was much more enjoyable as a result.

Use the knowledge below to inspire you to find your own 'natural' way of doing things. Try to find what feels right for you but what is also natural for us as humans. We are hardwired to breastfeed so we should be able to do it if we choose. Other questions I had were: "Aren't our bodies are designed to birth?" and "Was it meant to hurt?"

A Calmbirth® practitioner helped me. Kate Brereton is a mother of two, passionate about parents-to-be. She had much to 'calm' us about.

Kate says one of her proud moments in practice was when a father-to-be explained that he and his wife were really looking forward to their baby's birth day.

"In the Calmbirth® program, the woman will look forward to the day she births her baby. She will discover her inner capabilities and her resourcefulness even if unexpected challenges occur. Every birth journey is unique, no matter how it unfolds. There is no failure, it just is. Birth is a celebration of life and a new chapter of parents' lives."

Breathing And Visualisation Techniques

We found it was possible to create a bond with Calmbirth® techniques. Calmbirth® is an Australian registered and certified childbirth program that educates the birthing woman and her chosen support persons to use consciously controlled breathing techniques to help relax, and unify the mind and body during the birthing process.

There are so many negative stories around about birthing that surrounding yourself with some powerful positive ones can help you to prepare and relax in the last trimester.

Calmbirth® classes start at around 20-30 weeks and your partner can benefit from them too. You will be able to remove your old belief system that birth needs to be painful, dangerous, or requires medical management/intervention. This kind of birth is referred to as a disturbed birth, resulting in excessive muscle tension that results in more discomfort. C

Calmbirth® views the birth process as one where the woman trusts her body to release all the necessary hormones at the right time to support her body's natural, evolutionary ability to perform the ultimate creative female act – birth. She will accomplish more by doing less psychologically and physiologically, conserving energy to make sure she has reserves for birthing.

> **Calmbirth® therapy:**
> - Eliminates the fear and tension usually associated with giving birth, using relaxation.
> - Uses breathing techniques between uterine surges, known as 'waves'.
> - Uses consciously controlled breathing patterns.
> - Emphasises that the female body is designed to naturally give birth with ease and comfort.
> - Encourages your body's own natural pain relief — endorphins.
> - Creates a bond between mother and baby during pregnancy and afterwards.
> - Creates a calm serene, joyful experience with you, your partner and baby.
> - Allows you to gently breathe your baby into the world without the necessity of breath holding and pushing.

Make sure you find the right Calmbirth® practitioner for you. After all, they are just people and you may not resonate with the first one you find. It's very important you feel they are the right fit for you and your partner or support team.

Understanding what hormones will be released if you are relaxed is key. The knowledge that your body has all the right 'drugs' to help you through birth can be reassuring. It's when we don't understand that we may panic or fear. These negative emotions can cause the body to release adrenalin, which stalls dilation and makes it hard for oxytocin to be present. It may help you to know that a contraction is actually an opening (or at least a pushing down), not a closing. When you think of a muscle contraction, you may think of a tight shortening, but a birth contraction allows your stomach muscles to push your baby downward like a coffee plunger. You actually want the contractions to happen because with each contraction your baby is being pushed out. You work together as a team.

The bodily functions are involuntary, so you have no control over anything which is very scary for us Western women who want to be in control of everything. *Trusting* the bodily functions as natural, healthy and normal is paramount.

My husband cares for people with his hands, healing without drugs, surgery or medicine and is very much an advocate for natural health. So this is a philosophy we also apply to parenting. We feel we are natural parents, intuitive and very hands on. We believe this attitude came from our natural birth experience at the Monash Clayton birthing centre with only midwives and no intervention, allowing us to immediately connect with our baby. A natural birth sets up attached parenting foundations — we realised we are a family team working together. Our baby was helping us come out into the world and we knew from that moment on we needed to work together. With Warren in awe of my strength and me in awe of his support, we encountered a life experience that was actually amazing. We left as soon as we were allowed to, just 6 hours later and the birth centre midwives came to visit to check on me and help with breastfeeding.

A Natural Birth Day

The birth started with a toilet stop, which was part of the seven ritual visits before bed. This time was different. My bowels were clearing and I had strong 'period pain'. I really connected with what was happening to my body anatomically so I was able to switch off the 'pain'.

These were signs but I wasn't yet sure. I tried to sleep through it so that if it was our big day, I'd have energy for the marathon that lay ahead.

By 3am there was a pattern to these pains. They were contractions. Jan arrived to labour at home with us. We celebrated through the active labour, finally applying the TENS machine.

I remained calm, stretching and singing. I visualised the natural process, understanding my body was designed to birth. We were a team! Our baby was working with each contraction too. At 6am and 7cm dilated, we were ready for the birth centre. I waited for my waters to break.

I had a packed bag but no clothes to wear. I wanted to keep my dressing gown on. Jan asked: "Are you sick?" I replied: "No." She explained that only sick people wear dressing gowns to the hospital. I felt empowered and was reminded that I was well and healthy for birthing. But I insisted she take my dressing gown. Don't argue with a labouring woman!

Once we arrived, we made the room feel like ours. I moved in and out of being 'love drunk' to being primal. It was like having a big night out and not recalling what happened until someone reminded you the next day.

I could hardly talk, often wanting silence. I said "Jaaaannnn" in a slurred tone, overcome with love and relaxation. She replied: "Yes Andi."

"I love this TENS machine Jan. I love you but I love the TENS more." I was in love with everyone!

My birth plan included intervention only in an emergency, but when stage two labour kicked in, I momentarily doubted my ability to have a natural birth. I demanded pethidine and an epidural, grabbing on to Warren's t-shirt and telling him to forget the birth plan. But they knew I could do it and knew I may not respond well to those things so the birth centre midwives kept me active and got me back in 'the zone'. Baby had turned and disengaged slightly. They carefully assessed whether turning without intervention was possible.

All of a sudden, after an excruciating sensation of what felt like pressure against my organs, I learned that baby was turning and had the urge to push. "Jan, there's a foot in my diaphragm!" I shrieked. She replied: "Don't talk to me about it. Talk to your baby." Her subliminal message was to make me determined and bond with baby. Like an Amazonian warrior woman, I pushed the head out. I actually thought the midwives could grab it and pull the rest out. However, another big effort was needed and they asked me to touch the head. I reached down to feel. It was smooth. I began talking to the divine child realising we were a team and began bonding with baby once again. This gave me strength to have another push. With 51 minutes of pushing time and a labour of around 13 hours, our beautiful boy Beaudy (Beau) Shae Sipser was born. It was 2.21pm on January 3, 2010.

It was the hardest thing I've ever done, but the most empowering. Because my birth was natural, recovery was quicker and my pre-baby body returned within about a week with chiropractic care and breastfeeding, which also helped my uterus to contract to pre-pregnancy size.

Visits from midwives the next couple of mornings were amazing and the three of us are continuing to bond as a new family.

Preparing for Your Baby's Natural Birth Day

- **Change your perception about birth.** Know that it's <u>natural</u> and you are <u>safe</u> with the support team you have chosen.
- **Understand your anatomy.** Know that contractions are like an opening, not a closing and that with each contraction, it is pushing your baby down and helping you to birth baby, not hurting you.
- **Your baby is part of the team.** Connect with baby and remember how your divine child is there to help too.
- **Connect and bond with your baby at every opportunity.** Talk to your baby and when the head crowns, touch it.
- **Use distractions.** Use the TENS machine, a warm bath or shower and keep an article of your baby's clothing near you or hold it. You may even like to look at your ultrasound photo to keep you excited that soon you will be meeting your baby.

- **Lose control**. Let go and be in the moment. You are being guided by your body and baby, so trust it and breathe. Panicking causes different chemicals to be released, like adrenalin, making it harder.
- **Know that birthing may be emotionally challenging** because women's strongest feelings when giving birth, both positive and negative, focus on the way they were treated by their caregivers/parents. Use this time to do some healing in these relationships.
- **Make peace with your birth.** Know that your birth will be perfect for you. You cannot go wrong because there is no right or wrong in birthing. It's your very own personal and unique experience.

Your labour support team, which may consist of a partner, doula, private midwife, family members or friends, has a very big role — to be committed to providing you with support. Many don't know about the option of hiring a doula. The word 'doula' comes from ancient Greek and is now used to refer to a woman who helps another woman. It is a woman experienced in childbirth who provides physical, emotional and informational support to the mother before, during and just after childbirth.

Prepare a checklist like this for your birthing partner to go by during your labour:

- **Position** — is your partner moving and changing position often?
- **Urination** — is your partner going to the toilet every hour?
- **Relaxation** — is your partner as relaxed as possible? Are you allowing yourself to feel relaxed?
- **Respiration** — is she breathing deeply (please refer to Calmbirth® breathing techniques) Are you breathing in a calm pattern?
- **Rest** — is she taking advantage of the break between contractions? Refresh each other, both have sips of water, suck on ice or frozen fruit, have a damp cloth to wipe your and her face, massage her, have a stretch.
- **Reassurance** — are you encouraging and praising your partner? Seek support and advice from your midwife.

Birthing Partner Checklist
- Position
- Urination
- Relaxation
- Respiration
- Rest

Your Birth is Unique

No matter what happens, the old adage, "As long as mother and baby are safe and well", couldn't be more assuring. If you reach for the stars and land on the moon, it could be a really good ride. It's important to still go ahead with your birth plan and your ideal scenario. You at least get to enjoy the journey.

I had a friend who was really despondent because she had tried for a natural birth, did Calmbirth® classes, chiropractic care, ate really well throughout her whole pregnancy and was active and fit. Despite all of this, her baby's head was just too big and after many hours of trying, she just couldn't have a vaginal birth and intervention was necessary. Each case is so unique and yours will be too. The main thing to remember is that she didn't waste time, preparing for a natural birth for nothing. She really enjoyed her pregnancy and the journey. Imagine if she didn't do all of that pre-birth? Would it have been a worse outcome perhaps? But she gave it a good shot and they are both well and here.

It must be said though, that it is possible to address 'issues' and still have a vaginal and/or natural birth. With the right help, a vaginal/natural birth can be achieved no matter how big the head is in relation to the mother's pelvic outlet, or if it's a second pregnancy after a c-section. In my experience there are very few obstetricians that will help make this happen, but you can find them if that's what you want.

Benefits of Having a Natural Birth

As the baby passes through the vaginal canal, adrenalin is being built up and the baby gets to release this naturally as he tenses his muscles and pushes himself out.

The baby takes a huge gulp of amniotic fluid, which has a perfect pre-biotic and pro-biotic that prepares your baby's gut/digestive system.

If you do happen to have to have an emergency c-section, it's okay, because the safety of you and your baby is the main thing. Try to avoid an elective c-section. With any operation, healing does take time. Having a c-section may mean the difference between you recovering quicker, getting around faster or having an easier time getting breast milk to come through, because you may not need pain medications and other things as a result of the surgery.

After Birth Care

To continue a gentle and natural journey from birth, it's important to create a gentle transition for the baby from the womb to the world. There are three things to be aware of right after birth which you may like to explore more:

1. Don't cut the cord too soon

As well as a pulse in the cord after birth and vital nutrients being given to the baby, there's also an emotional connection between mother and baby via the cord. It's important to be aware of this and allow mother and baby decide when they are ready to be disconnected. We are too often in a clinical and controlled environment in hospitals, and unfortunately it doesn't allow for this natural and gentle transition to occur. Some mothers like to wait until the pulse in the cord has stopped or at least slowed down. It can be very traumatic for the baby and even the mother to clamp and cut the cord when there is still a life force flowing. The mother isn't always aware of these feelings as this is just the way it's done in Western society. But when we stop to actually think about it, it only makes sense to wait, bond and breathe then decide when the time is right for both of you. Some mothers have what is called a Lotus birth where they wait for the cord to fall off naturally, which is usually up to a few days after the birth. This practice is also known as nonseverance. Some cultures and species that practise nonseverance are some tribal aborigines, the Kalahari desert !Kung tribe, and some species of monkey like the chimpanzee. It can be quite traumatic for mother and baby to be detached too soon, or unnaturally. Even when the cord stops pulsing, it does not mean it has become useless along with the placenta. There is still blood flowing into the baby, and it is wise to wait until the child is finished with it. It provides Vitamin K and is rich in antibodies and nutrients. It has been suggested that babies who are born this way and are given the time to detach naturally don't suffer from Western illnesses such as colic or jaundice nearly as much.

A Lotus birth means your baby gets all the nutrition it needs naturally and you may decide to refuse the Hepatitis B and Vitamin K injections offered in a hospital at post natal care as a result. However, Dr Buckley explains it as more than just nutrition; it can be a very spiritual experience too. You may like to explore this option more.

My close friend is a veterinarian and television presenter. She saw first-hand just how traumatic it was when a ewe they had rescued was separated from her young. The ewe had been attacked by a dog and required urgent treatment. The two were temporarily separated while this was carried out. Despite her obvious pain and injuries, the frail mother cried out to the lamb, who replied with an equally desperate call. Their bleating became so distressing that the vets had no choice but to perform surgery with the youngster firmly by its mother's side. She noticed that even in the animal kingdom it's natural to have these instinctive feelings.

Medical doctor Sarah J. Buckley describes her experiences with Lotus birth.

Lotus Birth - A Ritual for Our Times
Dr. Sarah J. Buckley, MD

Lotus birth is the practice of leaving the umbilical cord uncut, so that the baby remains attached to his/her placenta until the cord naturally separates at the umbilicus - exactly as a cut cord does - at 3 to 10 days after birth. This prolonged contact can be seen as a time of transition, allowing the baby to slowly and gently let go of his/her attachment to the mother's body.

Although we have no written records of cultures which leave the cord uncut, many traditional peoples hold the placenta in high esteem. For example, Maori people from New Zealand bury the placenta ritually on the ancestral marae, and the Hmong, a hill tribe from South East Asia, believe that the placenta must be retrieved after death to ensure physical integrity in the next life: a Hmong baby's placenta is buried inside the house of its birth.

Lotus Birth is a new ritual for us, having only been described in chimpanzees before 1974, when Clair Lotus Day - pregnant and living in California - began to question the routine cutting of the cord. Her searching led her to an obstetrician who was sympathetic to her wishes, and her son Trimurti was born in hospital and taken home with his cord uncut. Lotus Birth was named by, and seeded through Clair to Jeannine Parvati Baker in the US and Shivam Rachana in Australia, who have both been strong advocates for this gentle practice.

Since 1974, many babies have been born this way, including babies born at home and in hospital, on land and in water, and even by caesarean section. Lotus birth is a beautiful and logical extension of natural childbirth, and invites us to reclaim the so-called third stage of birth, and to honour the placenta, our baby's first source of nourishment.

I am a New Zealand GP (family MD in America), and have 4 children born at home in my adopted country, Australia. I have experienced Lotus birth with my second and subsequent children, after being drawn to it during my second pregnancy through contact with Shivam Rachana at the Centre for Human Transformation in Yarra Glen, near Melbourne. Lotus birth made sense to me at the time, as I remembered my time training in GP obstetrics, and the strange and uncomfortable feeling of cutting through the gristly, fleshy cord that connects baby to placenta and mother. The feeling for me was like cutting through a boneless toe, and it felt good to avoid this cutting with my coming baby.

Through the CHT I spoke with women who had chosen this for their babies, and experienced a beautiful post-natal time. Some women also described their Lotus-Birth child's self-possession and completeness. Others described it as a challenge, practically and emotionally. Nicholas, my partner, was concerned that it might interfere with the magic of those early days, but was happy to go along with my wishes.

Zoe, our second child, was born at home on the 10th of September 1993. Her placenta was, unusually, an oval shape, which was perfect for the red velvet placenta bag that I had sewn. Soon after the birth, we wrapped her placenta in a cloth nappy, then in the placenta bag, and bundled it up with her in a shawl that enveloped both of them. Every 24 hours, we attended to the placenta by patting it dry, coating it liberally with salt, and dropping a little lavender oil onto it. Emma, who was 2, was keen to be involved in the care of her sister's placenta.

As the days passed, Zoe's cord dried from the umbilical end, and became thin and brittle. It developed a convenient 90 degree kink where it threaded through her clothes, and so did not rub or irritate her. The placenta, too, dried and shrivelled due to our salt treatment, and developed a slightly meaty smell, which interested our cat!

Zoe's cord separated on the 6th day, without any fuss; other babies have cried inconsolably or held their cord tightly before separation. We planted her placenta under a mandarin tree on her first birthday, which our dear friend and neighbour Annie later dug up and put in a pot when we moved interstate. She told us later that the mandarins from the tree were the sweetest she had ever tasted.

Our third child, Jacob Patrick, was born on the 25th September 1995, at home into water. Jacob and I stayed in the water for some time after the birth, so we floated his placenta in a plastic ice-cream carton (with the lid on, and a corner cut out for the cord) while I nursed him. This time, we put his placenta in a sieve to drain for the first day. I neither dressed nor carried Jacob at this time, but stayed in a still space with him, while Nicholas cared for Emma, 4, and Zoe, 2. His cord separated in just under 4 days, and I felt that he drank deeply of the stillness of that time.

His short "breaking forth" time was perfect because my parents arrived from New Zealand the following day to help with our household. He later chose a Jacaranda tree under which to bury his placenta at our new home in Queensland.

My fourth baby, Maia Rose, was born in Brisbane, where Lotus birth is still very new, on 26 July 2000. We had a beautiful 'Do It Yourself' birth at home, and my intuition told me that her breaking forth time would be short. I decided not to treat her placenta at all, but kept it in a sieve over a bowl in the daytime, and in the placenta bag at night. The cord separated in just under 3 days and, although it was a cool time of year, it did become friable and rather smelly. (Salt treatment would have prevented this). Maia's placenta is still in our freezer, awaiting the right time for burial, and I broke off a piece of her dried cord to give to her when she is older. My older children have blessed me with stories of their lives before birth, and have been unanimously in favour of not cutting the cord - especially Emma, who remembered the unpleasant feeling of having her cord cut, which she describes as being 'painful in my heart'. Zoe, at five years of age, described being attached to a 'love-heart thing' in my womb and told me "When I was born, the cord went off the love-heart thing and onto there (the placenta) and then I came out." Perhaps she experienced her placenta in utero as the source of nourishment and love.

Lotus birth has been, for us, an exquisite ritual which has enhanced the magic of the early post natal days. I notice an integrity and self-possession with my lotus-born children, and I believe that lovingness, cohesion, attunement to nature, trust, and respect for the natural order have all been imprinted on our family by our honouring of the placenta, the Tree of Life, through Lotus Birth.

The red velvet bag which I made for Zoe has been used for 20 more babies and I am happy to lend it out to local families.

Dr. Sarah J Buckley is a GP, mother of four children, and author of the internationally acclaimed book Gentle Birth, Gentle Mothering. *Her website, www.sarahbuckley.com is dedicated to gentle choices in pregnancy, birth and parenting.*

2. Do not bath your baby within the first 24 hours

Your baby has a protective coating around it after birth called the Vernix. It should be left on for around 24-48 hours as the baby is being moisturised and protected with vital nutrients that the skin (the largest organ in our body) needs. Contrary to most beliefs, it is not actually important to wash the baby straight after birth. In fact, not only is it drying, but it is emotionally trying. The baby has come from a very protected and safe environment and the change in texture and temperature can be traumatic. It's best to have a family bath with your baby, holding them close to you with a natural soap or no soap at all on day two or three. It is also unnecessary to bath your baby every day. Every second day is enough and you may decide to only wash the nappy area on alternate days.

3. Keep your baby close for breastfeeding

Keep your baby in the room with you and on you as much as possible. Some births don't always allow for this, like in some c-section deliveries, but you can make sure you have it written in your birth plan that you want to stay as near to your baby as possible, no matter what the outcome. It's crucial for bonding and milk supply. Also, make sure that when you are being taught how to breastfeed, that you feel the midwife is being gentle and respectful to you and your baby. No-one should touch your breasts and a very good lactation consultant will allow you and your baby to instinctively find each other and attach. If you don't have this experience, you may like to express your wishes and ask them to work with you, or find another lactation consultant. You will be able to learn more about breastfeeding in the chapters to come. But keep your baby on you and do not watch the clock; start to get to know your baby and his cues.

Whatever happens though, be proud of what you achieved and allow yourself time to heal from the birth both physically and emotionally. Get the right help around you to talk you through the ordeal. Then enjoy your blessing and bundle of joy and cut yourself some slack! You can still bond with your baby and there will be plenty of time for that; it may be more intense, but it's your own unique journey. Be proud no matter what outcome. It's important to feel empowered. Think of all the things you are grateful for as opposed to focusing on what you wished could have or should have happened. It is at this birthing time that a new mother needs to feel nurtured. Often a mother of a new baby needs to be mothered herself before she can mother her child. Birthing is always a big ordeal and probably the biggest thing that can happen to a woman. To feel is to heal. Allow yourself to cry. Don't berate yourself if you find that you feel upset. It is very normal. Talk about your feelings and ask for hugs and help.

Allow yourself to feel empowered. An empowered mother equals a calm child. Others can empower you by allowing you to find your own way and help you to listen to your intuition about what your baby needs. Your baby's needs are going to be a mixture of what you need too. After all, it is you two that are going to live together.

If you didn't have a vaginal birth and your baby missed out on the 'big gulp', there are still things you can do. You can get him checked by a chiropractor who deals with children to make sure their nervous systems are free of vertebral subluxation and realign cranial bones (in the skull), and you can arrange for pro-biotics for the gut. These and other immune-boosting things may help make up for a traumatic birth. The power of touch is very healing too and we will learn more about that in the chapters to come when we look at the benefits of massaging your baby. This will also help you and your baby to get better sleep.

Chapter Three

Why is My Baby Waking?

"Don't stand unmoving outside the door of a crying baby whose only desire is to touch you. Go to your baby. Go to your baby a million times. Demonstrate that people can be trusted, that the environment can be trusted, and that we live in a benign universe."

— Peggy O'Mara

The bottom line is babies are meant to wake frequently to be rocked and held. It's just the way we are designed. The movement is great for development of the vestibula part of the brain. My husband worked as a paramedic in Johannesburg, the most crime-filled city in the world besides a war zone, and there were many unwanted babies. He says that if the baby wasn't held or touched that after 2 weeks they failed to thrive. So this highlights how imperative touch is to the developing brain of a human. Rocking seems to be an innate need of babies and there is research that says it supports their development. So even waking to be rocked may mean they are using their innate intelligence for survival.

Nobody and nothing can prepare you for the sleep deprivation that lies ahead in the beginning of your new child's life. Many women think: "I didn't sign up for this", "How come nobody told me it was going to be this hard?" and "Don't I need to just train my baby to not wake?"

Paediatrician Dr. Sears suggests otherwise:

> "One thing we have learned during our years in paediatrics is that babies do what they do because they're designed that way. In the case of infant sleep, research suggests that active sleep protects babies. Suppose your baby sleeps

like an adult, meaning predominantly deep sleep. Sounds wonderful! For you perhaps. But not for a baby. Suppose baby had a need for warmth, food, or even unobstructed air, but because he was sleeping so deeply he couldn't arouse to recognise and act on these needs. Baby's well-being could be threatened. It appears that babies come wired with sleep patterns that enable them to awaken in response to circumstances that threaten their well-being. We believe, and research supports, that frequent stages of active (REM) sleep serve the best physiologic interest of babies during the early months, when their well-being is most threatened."[1]

You'll get an understanding of the way the human brain works and how similar it is to the reptilian brain. We are, after all mammals and pack animals and when we liken our behaviours and brain to the animal kingdom, the baby waking activity will make sense, as it's natural evolutionary survival programming. Our brains are just like that of our fellow mammals. We humans are a species that is prone to predation at night. We are designed to keep our young close and wake frequently for protection from animals that are a threat to us such as a lion that may come to eat us. If a baby or 'young' cries, it is a threat to the community, so we are hardwired to keep them within arm's reach and offer the breast. Even though we live in safe houses in a modern world and the way we live has changed; the way our brains are designed has not, so to be left alone at night for a baby is really scary until they have motor skills that mean they can fend for themselves.

Imagine you were still growing at a rapid rate. If I grew out of a size in weeks or months, I too would probably wake all night to feed. If I was alone in a room on a flat still bed with no noise of heartbeats and organs and no movement, I too would wake all night.

The difficult part is that we do not live in the world with only primal needs of eating, sleeping and basic survival skills that are necessary for co-existing with the animal kingdom and other mammalian species. In Western society we have eschewed the mammalian way of looking after children. We do not always trust our biological and hormonal instincts to keep our young close and live far away from each other in big houses with no support from the rest of the 'village'. We have jobs and operate heavy machinery like driving cars and therefore our brains need to be very switched on so that we don't cause an accident. We cannot afford to be tired. It would be dangerous, right?

---

1 Dr Sears *8 Infant Sleep Facts Every Parent Should Know*

But we are working against the natural way we are meant to live and rear our young so we can adapt to the environment around us. This is why there are challenges. If we lived in Africa or some other parts of the globe, it may be easier or at least feel more natural. However, the 'modern day parent' can find a middle ground. It is possible work with the natural waking activity of a healthy baby and still manage to get some sleep and be healthy ourselves.

Know that you can have it all; just not all at once. The following chapters will get you through the wakeful times of being a new parent; they will help you get all the sleep you need to be healthy and function well. It is possible when you're committed and creative!

Rules And Truths

- It's normal for babies to wake at night.
- The truth is that babies only have two stages of sleep, whereas adults have three. It's very normal for them to only sleep in 40 minute sleep cycles and any more than 2 hours in a row is unusual.
- Until the child's brain is mature and fully developed, your baby will need you to help him get back to sleep.
- Being a responsive parent sets up neurological pathways that help fully develop your baby's brain and create a child who is more contented during the day and more emotionally available to life.
- Research shows that night waking is healthy for development and any sort of sleep training is very stressful for babies and their psychological health.
- If you intuitively feel there is something else 'wrong', consider having your baby's nervous system and spine checked by a chiropractor who is used to looking after babies.

In our book *7 Things Your Doctor forgot to Tell You*, we talk about symptoms being a sign to change and improve our health. Sometimes if you didn't have the warning sign, you wouldn't do anything about it and make a change. So we refer to the problem actually sometimes being the solution. For instance, having angina (chest pain) may force you to stop smoking. Let's look at vomiting. While it's not comfortable, if the reason why you are vomiting is because you ate rotten food, then the problem is the solution. Your body recognises that it doesn't want that rotten food in your system so it gets rid of it through an orifice; if not first the mouth then maybe through the other end. The healthier you are, the quicker your expulsion will be. Some may develop a rash and expel through the largest organ and smallest orifices in our body — the pores.

Okay, so this is a massive concept but if this makes sense to you now, you'll be able to see that a baby that the 'problem' of a baby that wakes often, may sometimes be the solution. In fact if there's no pathology and disease, or vertebral subluxation stopping them from expressing their full potential then you have a very healthy baby. I hear lots of mums say the wakeful ones are the clever ones! How much would you like to support your baby's endeavours to be clever?

I use this analogy about wakeful babies and compared the 'problem' to the way it felt when my baby was up all night when I was pregnant. He would kick and turn and play skipping rope with the umbilical cord. Then he would roll like a dolphin when the moon was full and finally when there wasn't much room, he'd twist his hands and push his feet into my diaphragm. He was so active that my husband, drawing on his experience as pediatric chiropractor, would explain to me that an active baby is a healthy one. You see, movement runs the brain. That's why when you have an accident the best thing to do is keep your body moving so the brain never switches off. A physical therapist in a hospital is hired to come and move your legs. This is why chiropractic care is so beneficial to improving health. When you take the pressure off your life line — your brain and spinal cord and the nerves that branch off — you send healthier signals to the rest of the body and allow for better movement, expansion and contraction of muscles and organs, which are muscles too. So when a baby moves in the womb, it's good for the developing nerve system of that baby. It was reassuring knowing that my baby was active inside me and while some may find it hard to sleep with the movement, I slept better while he kicked all night because I knew he was there and healthy! So here's the light at the end of the 'for crying out loud' tunnel — If babies are wakeful, they are active. If they are active, it's great for the nerve system development, which is, believe it or not, still developing! In fact, some babies will stir or cry in the night to get your attention so you will pick them up and rock them back to sleep. They want the rocking because it's movement and that movement is great for a part of the developing brain called the cerebellum.

So once we make peace with having a wakeful baby and understand that it's healthy and there's no problem and that you haven't done anything wrong, you can then relax and find a way to get some rest yourself. You see, I wasted so much time arguing and researching and justifying and wondering what was happening. It served me so I could research and write this book and help you, but if I could save you the hours of sleep deprivation and heartache, I'll die happy. Don't waste another minute now.

Ok, so we understand babies don't need the kind of sleep an adult does. What about the mother? Does she need the same sleep she had before? There's a type of sleep that will help you cope and carry on, which I'll reveal. I'm going to give you the tools you need to get the quality sleep you need to carry on through the tough first couple of years. Prior to realising that a wakeful baby is healthy, a new mother may be up all night or filled with anxiety wondering what she did wrong or trying to solve the problem when there may not actually be one. Once you have had baby checked for pathology by a doctor and then a chiropractor for vertebral subluxation that may have resulted from birth or in utero, which may have caused your baby to be unsettled, you know the wakefulness is healthy sign.

Healthy reasons why your baby is wakeful:
- Too hot
- Too cold
- Temperature regulation
- Teething discomfort
- A soiled nappy
- The urge to urinate
- Needing to be rocked to stimulate the developing brain and be reminded of the safety of the womb
- Wind
- Burps
- Sore tummy from learning how to digest new food
- Intolerance to certain foods or chemical smells
- Terrified by the unfamiliar and foreign world around them
- Scared of the silence at night when they are used to a noisy womb
- Frightened of being away from the caregiver because they cannot fend for themselves if a lion comes and get them in the night. They are acting according to primal instincts and don't know that we live in the 21st century in big safe houses. Mammalian species (except humans) keep their young close and so to be apart can be unsettling as the young can't fend for themselves and rely on the mother to be at arm's reach and protect them. They, if compared to the animal kingdom, will keep completely still to be extremely quiet so that the predator won't find them. They end up so quiet that they are feigning death and eventually fall asleep; not from feeling relaxed but rather the opposite, feeling exhausted. They release

excess cortisol from so much adrenalin that this is actually damaging to psychological development too.

- The need to hear the heart beat and fall asleep to that rhythm, or synchronise breathing as the mammalian species do. You will often only fall asleep once you and your bed partner have synchronised breathing, and heart beats too.
- The startle reflex means they accidently hit themselves in the face and they may not know yet that it is their limbs.
- Hungry
- Thirsty
- Over-handled in the day, over tired or over-stimulated, therefore agitated
- Needing immune cells from breast milk to fight off an illness
- Fighting off any disease and feeling uncomfortable as a result
- Wanting a hug
- Different developmental stages where they are becoming more aware of the world around them. (This can often happen at 6 weeks when they can see more of the world and eyesight is improving. It also happens around 6-8 months where they are teething and crawling and may have started eating solids.)
- Knowing you need a hug and wanting to give you one too.
- Stimulation of milk supply — relaxing you so you can make better breast milk and produce prolactin, which is a hormone released by the pituitary gland that stimulates breast development and milk production in women.
- Staying near so your hormones continue to supply breast milk and or breastfeed to help you fall asleep.
- Your baby rejected your breast milk because you drank alcohol or is stimulated from caffeine or drugs you consumed.
- Your baby needs a top up of breast milk because it has a tiny stomach and is growing at a rapid rate. Breast milk is designed to be highly digestible. This is so that the digestive system doesn't need to work very hard so that the nervous system can fully develop. It moves straight through them so frequent feeding is necessary, even if you just fed them. This top up may in fact be the hind milk which is rich in essential fatty acids needed for a deep sleep
- Night terrors. (Avoid television with violent or fast images in the background).

- The end of a sleep cycle. Babies only sleep 40 minutes to 2 hours (three sleep cycles) at a time. Breast-fed babies usually sleep for one longer stretch in the 24-hour period. This usually coincides with the lunar cycle and will be when you first put them down at night for 4-5 hours. If your baby is sleeping for a 4-5 hour stretch in one 24-hour period, it's completely normal and healthy and will usually be after a cluster feed. (Where your baby feeds regularly and often before a big sleep). The research around REM (rapid eye movement) sleep explains that we should view night waking in a baby as completely normal and healthy.
- The best advice I can give is to make sure you are going to sleep at this time too. It may be hard going to bed at 7pm or 8pm, because you may like to have time with your partner. Try doing so at least three nights a week and make the other four nights for them. Having a four-hour stretch at this time of night will do you wonders.

We need to trust that our baby's reason for waking is valid for them. So if we take every single one of these reasons into consideration, we can understand that it's normal for babies to have woken from at least two or more of these reasons every night.

There are probably many more reasons your baby may wake but it's important to set the record straight right now: wakeful babies are not only normal, but they're also healthy.

Dr. Sarah J. Buckley states: "One of the problems that our culture creates for new mothers is the belief that infant sleep is, or should quickly become, the same as adult sleep." This misinformed goal can cause much suffering for the mother, baby and whole families when they try to fix the 'problem'. A baby's central nerve system, in particular the brain, is 75% smaller than an adult's. Higher brain function has not been established. Unlike most other mammalian species that can move away from a threat almost from birth, human babies cannot and require more parental care and closer proximity to the carer than any other species.

It should now be easier to see that your little person is actually doing it tough and relies on you to gently help them get used to the world around them in the safety of your arms, in close proximity to their food and life supply. Some mothers have the theory that babies don't realise they are separate from the mother until after nine months. Many say this is when huge separation anxiety can occur. However, there can be bouts of separation anxiety through each psychological development phase. They just need you more for the first nine months.

I like to view the waking as a chance for them to be held again. If you don't co-sleep, your baby may wake to be touched, skin to skin, because it's this kind of touch that stimulates the release of oxytocin, (the love hormone) which will ensure you are still in love with your child.

Sleep Myths

"If there is anything we wish to change in the child, we should first examine it and see whether it is not something that could better be changed in ourselves."

— Carl G. Jung

MYTH
Babies are meant to be trained to 'sleep through'

TRUTH

For the reasons I've outlined earlier, this is clearly not true. Yet there is one statement on the lips of every parent and is the most common question asked of new parents: "Is your baby sleeping through yet?"

The most a health new born or toddler breast fed baby will usually sleep in one go is 4-6 hours. This is usually after a cluster feed. A cluster feed is so common and healthy and will happen at the same time within a 24-hour period. A cluster feed is frequent feeds, including top-ups where the baby falls asleep on the breast, only to wake sometimes 20 minutes later to get more milk and fall back into a deeper sleep. Most of the time this happens when you first put them to sleep at night to coincide with the lunar cycle and cycadian rhythm.

So if your baby is doing a 5-hour stretch, you can proudly say to anyone who asks, "Yes, my baby sleeps very well".

Any sort of strict 'baby training' can be very damaging to the developing brain and should be a subject approached with caution.

Sleep training is only a relatively new and modern concept. It was developed by Luther Holt, a popular doctor in the late 19th century who explained to mothers that they should not display too much affection and closeness to their child when they cried. Child experts these days have moved away from such theories, explaining that motherly love is in fact the key ingredient needed to settle a baby.

"This generation of mothers labor under the dubious pronouncement that babies sleep best in isolation. Every infant knows better. His protest at nocturnal solitude contains the wisdom of millennia" (Thomas Lewis MD, via Elizabeth Pantley).

MYTH
If your baby isn't 'sleeping through', it's unhealthy for you and the baby

TRUTH
Many doctors and others may tell you that it's unhealthy if your baby isn't sleeping from 7pm–7am or something similar. They're usually talking from a nutritional perspective and may see many bottle-fed babies whose stomachs are wiped out by the formula they've been fed and may not need to feed again if they wake. People assume that babies only wake for one reason — to feed. So they figure if they're warm, safe, burped and changed then they certainly don't need to be fed again and should be 'trained' into not waking. You can rest assured that in time, your baby's brain will develop and he'll learn naturally how to fall asleep for longer periods by himself. If you follow your child's lead and help them fall back to sleep during a sleep cycle, you could be reaping the rewards later.

For the mother, the myth surrounding the notion that it's unhealthy if the mother doesn't get 8 hours sleep like before the birth is unfounded. While it's important for mothers to get good sleep, the type of sleep you get is different. It's really amazing how when you breastfeed, your hormones can actually allow you to get the quality sleep you need to function well. And quality doesn't necessarily equal quantity. Another common phrase is: "sleep when the baby sleeps." This is very true. Whether or not you breastfeed, if you follow your baby's sleep patterns, you most certainly will get the right amount of sleep you need.

MYTH
You need to sleep all night like you used to

TRUTH
If you entertain the notion that you will not be getting much sleep in the night at first then maybe you will be more committed to having day naps. Make peace with this transitional period of your new person's life and find creative ways to work with it.

Viewing it as a problem or something you need to fix may only leave you feeling upset or frustrated. You will be able to function really well if you can follow your baby's sleep patterns in the day too. You may need to make sure there is nothing to do before you feed so you can fall asleep the same time as your baby. There's nothing more unsettling than trying to feed someone to sleep and all the while you are thinking about those last few emails that need to be sent once 'baby is down'. Once you get started on those emails, it will be hard for you to switch off and take a nap. Make the most of the relaxed feeling of accomplishment you get once your baby is asleep and go to sleep too.

The other way you can get really good sleep is to go to sleep early at night, when your baby does. Now for some mothers who have other children, this may be nearly impossible but if there are two or three nights a week where someone else in your family can take care of things while you have an early night even if it is just those few times a week, you'll find your energy levels will really improve. It really can make a difference because that's when your baby will usually do his longest stretch of sleep too. If it is your only child, try to bath and eat with them so that you can peacefully fall asleep when they do. There will be time to work, bond with your partner or watch TV. It just may not be at the times you were used to doing it all. Your schedule just changes for a little while as your baby and your family adjust.

MYTH
You need to limit the amount of times your baby wakes to feed

TRUTH
It is now known that high levels of melatonin in breast milk appear during the night and low levels during the day. Since melatonin is the hormone that regulates the sleep/wake cycle, these changes in breast-milk will doubtless be the signal to help the baby adapt as quickly as possible to the day/night versus sleep/wakefulness environment. This shows another reason why it's all such a natural act and way of parenting; gentle for the both of you. So try not to put up a fight at the amount of times your baby wakes to feed. It may be to help you sleep deeper, for the baby to get some analgesic properties from the milk, or all the other reasons we've covered. After you have tried rocking, cuddling, burping and have ruled out any possible signs of ill health, you can be sure that breastfeeding your baby back to sleep will be the easiest way for all parties to get some sleep!

Nurturing your baby to be self-reliant

From the first day your baby enters this world he is learning from you, primarily, how to make choices. He either learns to listen to himself or seeks cues from others around him. When your baby signals to you and receives a prompt response, he learns to rely on himself because it's working for him. A child who is used to making choices about himself based on parental coercion will do the same with peer pressure later in life. If we direct the child's personal choices, we take him away from independence and teach him to follow others, even against his own wisdom. This can relate to sleeping choices and views on teaching a baby to 'self- settle'. Is the baby who sleeps alone and on their own developing more independence? Actually the answer is no. Because he is left to cry himself to sleep alone, he will eventually sleep, but his ability to rely on himself has been eroded. Your baby is actually learning to succumb to the will of others and become dependent on cues from outside himself. The self-settling and sleeping alone arrangement happens in negation to his own need if he has called for you and you don't succumb. He is giving up his independent choice and is in fact learning to be dependent. If the parent follows the baby's lead of wanting to be close during sleep and near his mother's body, the baby is peaceful and feeling right about following his inner voice.

There were days when my son would insist on me not letting him go when I was about to put him back in his bed. His arm would be draped around my neck. As I gently slid my own arm from under his neck, his arm would draw me in tighter as though he was indicating that he didn't want me to go. I felt the cold space between us and understood what it must be like for him. On other days he even chose to just be in the same room as me while he played. I likened it to how ducks are when they waddle with their little ducklings. They followed their mama around in a line. They seem to not only enjoy being close but do it because it's innate. His *choice to stay close to me was an independent choice.* I respected him totally. He is already growing up to be extremely social and incredibly independent in every way. At the end of the day, the happy balance is when the child is rooted in himself with such confidence that he is free to choose. Independence comes at various stages for such unique little people. You must have confidence and trust within yourself that this will happen. People say that you do not always end up teaching your children everything. They teach you things too. Here's a powerful example of how your child may be teaching you independence by trusting him. Without self-doubt, you would realise that the word, "clingy" is an emotionally loaded judgment, suggesting something is wrong. In reality, your son prefers to be with you much of the time. How wonderful for him and for you.

Chapter Four

No Cry Babies

"If we were all first-time parents isolated on a deserted island without the advice of baby books, doctors, psychologists or in-laws, you would care for your child instinctively — breastfeeding, holding and carrying your baby during the day and sleeping with your baby in the night."

— Dr William Sears

By the time a baby cries, it has had to work itself up so much that stress hormones have been released and it's really traumatic for them. Adrenalin will be released, which leads to a flooding of cortisol in the body. This negatively impacts on normal and healthy function. These chemicals should only be released in response to a significantly stressful event and the less this cascade is accessed, the better the baby's health will be.

From womb until the age of 6 months is when our nerve system develops. At age five we are still being programmed by our surroundings. What is our baby learning if we don't attend to its needs at night? There's a myriad research on 'controlled' crying' and 'cry it out methods', why it doesn't work or the psychological issues it may create, with the toddler having tantrums and experiencing feelings of abandonment and adults being prone to depression. It's important to know that despite the myths and misconceptions that it's "healthy for a baby to cry and exercise its lungs", it's actually very much the opposite and very unhealthy to be in this stress response. By helping your baby through their 'big' feelings, you are helping your baby's brain wire correctly and giving them coping strategies as an adult. They are also learning they don't need to get dramatic and try really hard to get your attention. They learn and trust that you will be there for them if they need you. This trust bond will pay off as you start to notice your child feels more secure to play alone in the day. He has learnt he can explore more and be on his own, because if something should happen, you will respond. By the time the frontal lobe of their developing brain has finished wiring, you've helped your baby as a child and then as an adult to handle stressful and emotional situations in an optimal way. The brain is at its most plastic (can change the most) in this early stage and emotional adaptation is forever imprinted from this time.

It's an investment that's a small price to pay if you want to avoid things like the 'terrible two' stage and better interaction with others and siblings.

Like adults, babies take in their surroundings, only more so. From the time we enter this world, we are learning. We have come out of a nice warm womb, with our food 'on tap' via the umbilical cord and then into a cold, bright detached environment where we must learn to ask for our food. Crying is the last sign a baby uses to ask for food. Not the first. There are so many other cues — like hand to mouth and arching to the side — that we can miss because we are too busy looking at the clock to calculate when the last feed was, instead of looking to what our little person's needs are on that particular day.

Very few mums express enthusiasm about letting their baby cry themselves to sleep. Most mothers explain that it breaks their heart to hear it or how they wish they could pick their baby up. It makes sense that it doesn't feel right and that there had to be another solution to helping babies sleep. I know even though some mums say it breaks their hearts to do it, that after 'x' amount of nights of hearing their baby scream, that their baby never did it again and 'slept through'.

Babies only have two stages of sleep unlike adults who have three. As a health author and certified infant massage instructor, I understand the psychological ramifications and have since learnt that because it is so exhausting and really stressful to keep crying that hard, it's better to not call out anymore. After all the exhausting crying, they then feign death, as though in the animal kingdom.

Humans are a part of the animal kingdom and in terms of the food chain, prone to predation at night. This fact has been a constant for millennia. Our brains are designed to wake frequently for many reasons like breathing and temperature regulation and rocking for vestibular development. Our milk is similar to that of a monkey, with 40/60 fat ratio and highly digestible, therefore we need to wake frequently to feed and be within arm's reach of our parents. As a result, a cry or stressed sound from a baby at night will alert predators, which increases the likelihood of being attacked. For this reason, infants close to their milk supply and or carer are less likely to call out or cry out. Thus the species (humans) have survived. The only circumstance that has changed is that we don't have wild animals around, but the baby's response to stress is the same because our DNA response is geared for survival. So a baby subjected to controlled crying is still waking, but not calling out; instead feigning death (going silent), so the animal/predator cannot find them.

I knew I didn't want to teach or program my baby that I wasn't going to be there for him when he needed me. I've never been okay with my baby learning that if he cries, I will not come. His cries are about feeling unsafe and needing to be close, which is age appropriate because he cannot fend for himself. His still-developing brain does not have the wiring yet to understand such a concept so it sounds very healthy for him to behave this way. The frontal lobe of his brain is still wiring. He is behaving in a purely primal manner.

> **If you leave your baby to cry to sleep in his room, the car or pram:**
> - High levels of toxic stress hormones and excess adrenalin and cortisol are released.
> - A withdrawal of opioids, which promote feelings of wellbeing, occurs in your baby's brain.
> - This stress response can hardwire a baby for oversensitivity for life.
> - Pain circuits in the brain become activated so your child thinks they have been hurt physically.

If you have felt okay with letting your child cry to sleep, it may be because you didn't understand what happens to a baby's brain.

Your Child Has Three Brains

Because your child is still developing, how you parent is paramount to the impact on his emotional well-being.

Your child's three brains are working together in harmony but at times, one part is dominant.

1. The Rational Brain

This refers to the frontal lobes or the neo-cortex. Neo, meaning new, it can be referred to as the newest part of the brain and also forms the majority (About 85%

of the total mass). It envelopes the mammalian and reptilian parts and is responsible for creativity, imagination, problem solving, reasoning/reflection, and kindness or empathy for others. Imagine what this part of the brain is capable of: great things towards other humans. But when this part is cut off from the other part of the brain — the mammalian brain's social emotional systems — it can also be responsible for terrible cruelties.

2. The Mammalian Brain

This part of the brain can be known as the emotional brain, which is the lower part and is just like other mammals' brains such as monkeys. It can trigger strong emotions that must work together with, and be managed by, the rational brain to control things like the fight or flight impulses generated by the nervous system in times of perceived stress. It activates rage, fear, separation distress, caring and nurturing, exploration and playfulness, and in adults, this part of the brain is responsible for lust.

3. The Reptilian Brain

This part of the brain is the most ancient as it is largely unchanged by evolution and activates primal types of behaviour related to survival. It also controls essential bodily functions like breathing, digestion, hunger, movement, posture and balance, as well as temperature. It blends in to the brain stem, which then transcends into the spinal cord, which is protected by the bones of the spine/vertebrae. Making sure these bones are in a correct alignment from birth is good for optimal function and development.

Will misalignment of the spine or the way you parent make such an impact on your child's developing nervous system that it makes one part of the brain more active than the others? Will one part of the brain become more dominant? Could your child become programmed to respond in fight or flight because the reptilian brain keeps triggering primitive and primal instincts to defend or attack? Acting on a primal level, he may feel so much hurt that he adapts by cutting off feelings of love and need in the mammalian part of his brain and ends up in life over-rationalising and never really being able to form close relationships.

When the three brains work in harmony and in a balanced way, he is able to enjoy life with a fully wired and developed human brain reaching higher levels of social and emotional intelligence, allowing him to express a greater level of concern for others and compassion towards all living things.

CHAPTER FOUR - NO CRY BABIES

Since most of the human brain develops after birth with rapid growth over the next five years of your child's life, you have much influence on your child's higher unfinished brain.

It's because the higher part of your baby's brain is unfinished that the lower brain takes control. This is why you may notice severe stress if your baby is hungry, tired, too cold or too hot, or experiencing other primitive impulses. As a toddler, they may cry and roll around on the floor, express anger and scream. This is not a 'naughty' child. It is a child with a brain that is still developing and acting primal. When your child has these feelings, the lower brain is operating at full throttle; it's in fifth gear because the higher brain structures are still underdeveloped. Your child does not know yet how to calm themselves down and relies on you to help. Not responding allows their brains to stay in mid-brain overdrive, which is very stressful for them.

How you help and act with understanding and empathy can make a massive impact and help wire their brain. Attending to your child with a gentle voice and helping them through these overwhelming feelings can set up essential brain pathways that will eventually help him to learn how to calm himself. The key part to remember here is the 'attending' part. Attending to your child is key. Then how you attend is just as important.

Because you now have a level of understanding, it should be easy to attend to your child with an empathetic type of love and allow a release of oxytocin (love hormone). If you don't attend to your baby, down play or criticise your child for these feelings, you block the release of these love hormones. If this happens, the brain can feel it is in a stressed state causing the lower brain to be overactive in life later on. This may mean they become angry too easily, worried and over-reactive. Research shows that quality of life is dramatically affected by not creating stress-regulating systems in the childhood brain.

Criticism such as "You shouldn't always attend to your child", no longer made sense. We didn't even question it anymore, no matter how tired we were, because we had the knowledge that the child's brain was different to the adult brain. Statements like; "You are spoiling your child", or "You aren't teaching them resilience", now sounded not only naïve, but ludicrous. But it wasn't their fault. Like us, they too just didn't have the knowledge we now have about a child's unfinished three brains.

Many depressed people I have known feel they are unsupported. This wasn't always necessarily true because the support is there, but that's their perception. I sometimes wonder if these feelings stemmed from being programmed as a baby — were their parents there for them when they needed them?

I wanted our child to know his feelings were valid no matter what age. I wanted him to know that I had 'his back'. It was going to be a tough and long road as a sleep-deprived new mum recovering from a birth, but the effort was going to pay off. It already has. I see how happy he is to play and explore on his own.

Babies that weren't subjected to controlled crying were shown to be more adventurous and able to learn faster.

The Study of Love
Introducing Attachment Theory

When a baby cries, that is an 'attachment behaviour'. When a parent has a pattern of responding to that cry, the baby knows that he is safe. But when a parent has a pattern of responding differently, such as not coming, or coming inconsistently, then the baby knows that his survival may be on the line. It is at this point that a baby knows he must either increase or change the signal to get help.

You can see that the way in which the parent responds to their baby will create the pattern that the child must match in order to ensure his survival.

If you are a new parent of a little baby you may hear the advice, 'That's no way to stop him crying, you're just rewarding him by picking him up'. And the advice sounds convincing, but not if you are using the attachment perspective and empathising with your baby.

What you can say is, 'Let's look at this from the baby's perspective'.

He can't meet his own needs and needs me to do things for him. Even if I don't pick him up, he is still going to be needing me. So to get my attention he's going to have to get more and more upset, and eventually I will pick him up.

So if I don't pick him up I'm training him to get very upset immediately because nothing else works to get my attention. If he can't trust me to fulfil his needs, then he'll stick close to me because he won't trust me when I'm out of his sight. That means he'll explore less and won't develop so many skills. And my baby will turn into a whingeing, clingy pre-schooler.

Or perhaps I could follow your advice and not pick him up at all when he cries. How would that turn out? Looking at it from my baby's perspective, he still needs me, but obviously, his cries disturb me so much that I can't respond. To make me feel safe he'll have to pretend that he has no emotional needs. He'll learn to switch them off. And then he won't be able to recognise them in other people either. My baby will turn into a preschooler who won't have the empathic skills needed to make friends.

But if I do pick him up, he learns that empathy is seeing how someone feels and valuing that in your actions. He'll know that I'm always going to be there to meet his needs and he will soon discover that it isn't necessary to get upset and cry to get his needs met. So, eventually, when he wants me, he'll just call out once and wait. Because he trusts me he'll turn into a happy little explorer because he knows Mum will be there watching and protecting. He will develop lots of the skills needed for independence. And my baby will grow into an independent, sociable and cheerful preschooler.

While studying at university, researchers believed that the active, the *magic*, ingredient for child development was 'stimulation'. "Is your baby getting enough stimulation?" was the question you were likely to be asked by the health professionals. But it was the wrong question.

We were doing all the right things with our babies by playing, touching, kissing, holding, singing to, talking to and cuddling them, but the most important thing in doing all this was *not* stimulation. It was the fact that this playful interaction built the knowledge that mother and child had of each other and strengthened the emotional connection - the *attachment* - between them.

Babies that were control cried sometimes looked 'emotionally unavailable' author and mentor Pinky McKay would point out. I began to notice that they would often cry when passed to another person in the day. It was as though they were confused or needed more hugs from mum. They were going to be attached to their mother and love her but they were constantly *insecure* in their attachment. I observed that babies that were responded to every time they needed were *secure* in their attachment to their parents.

Book Extract from **Raising the Best Possible Child** ***by Jo Jackson King.***

Every time your baby wakes or cries out, I guarantee, it's for a reason. Whether it's to regulate body temperature, burp or feel your heart beat, that reason is valid for them at that time and always age appropriate. There is so much pressure to have babies sleep with an adult sleep cycle too soon, which only leaves the mother, or father, feeling inadequate when this doesn't happen.

Have you ever woken up at night to empty your bladder and felt annoyed but then kept lights off and gently crawled back in to bed to 'spoon' your partner and fall back to sleep? Some babies can wake each time they have to urinate or even fart. Just like you, it can wake them, so there are so many factors that can wake your healthy baby. These things are out of your control, but will eventually stop in time. This book is about being patient and understanding the benefits of helping your baby get back to sleep upon waking, with gentle ways of doing so and without any unnecessary crying. Babies have enough to adapt to as its tiny digestive system prepares, or it slowly learns that it is no longer attached to you; so gently helping them to sleep without the need for crying to get your attention for help is your gift to your darling angel, your little person, your miracle you made! By doing so, you're ensuring your baby's needs are met on both an emotional and physical level, which allows for optimum development. The most rewarding part is that you create a loving bond for life!

Parenting and Riots - A 'Cry' For Help

As a new mother, the riots in London in August 2011 got me watching the news with different eyes. I wanted to listen to what these people, —each someone's child— had to say. They were torn, hurt, angry and looking for attention. In interviews, they explained it was the only way to make the government listen to their message, which was a call or 'cry' for change.

The Guardian brigade saw it as social protest; the Daily Mail brigade saw it as criminal outrage.

I explored the damage to the child, who is now an adult, inflicted by lack of nurture. When does parenting stop? At the age of 18? Surely not. Surely it's a role that continues for the rest of our lives.

I said to my husband Warren that night: "There are other ways of getting attention. Protest with balloons being let off in the air simultaneously, or line up nude with signage. Others have been known to go on hunger strikes. These kinds of world-making news protests don't harm others."

It made me feel really sorry for these rioters. Their actions were wrong, but they were experiencing real, raw emotion. Were these acts of violence from babies who had been left to cry? Did these babies become adults who, just as all the literature and research explains in the book *The Science of Parenting* by Margot Sunderland, became adults who were left with feelings of depression and other psychological problems? Have they been taught and programmed with this type of parenting that in stressful times the only way to get attention is to do something extreme, because when you ask nicely, nobody listens anyway?

These could have been the babies that proponents of the strict routine described as 'naughty' babies. Yet, were they? Or are they just all people with a birth right to be loved and nurtured no matter what time of day or night? Were these the babies that ended up vomiting to get their parents' attention after crying didn't work? Some authors, I was really disturbed to learn, recommended leaving vomit towels in and around the cot because you must teach your 'naughty baby' that it's not a way to get attention.

The author, book or anyone really who tells us this behaviour is okay, is someone who foolishly believes that babies can be 'trained' into sleeping. They have ignored all the research on babies' brains and the science of how it works. They are so desperate for sleep and 'buy into' a lie that helps them cope.

If you choose to control cry your baby or let it cry to sleep, I shall not judge you. I believe you are doing whatever you can to get through and 'save' your family. I do feel sorry for those who gain information from 'authorities' like these authors and baby trainers though who aren't privy to the information or responsible enough to share the sometimes chilling ramifications.

Emotional development from such a young age is crucial, based on scientific research. Neuronets are forming during babyhood. The frontal lobe of a child's brain is not wired properly until around the age of 5. "Give me the child until he is seven and I will show you the man." (Saint Ignatius of Loyola, Founder of the Society of Jesus/the Jesuits)

Current day parenting manuals and doctors encourage a technique that leaves brain damage at the emotional level — with chilling consequences. Brain damage is literally inflicted by 'controlled crying', which means abandonment, despair, and detachment, and is often diagnosed as depression, anxiety or attachment disorder in children as young as 6 or 7.

Is anyone else concerned by this? It is this sort of 'joined–up' thinking that sheds light on how we were brought up and the emotional consequences. Perhaps we can break the pattern.

It may not be the only cause of the riots — very few people would accept it as such — but I bet this is a contributing factor. I'd add that the socially accepted norm of giving children as young as 4 war games, slasher movie computer games as 'entertainment' or 'to keep them quiet' or taking them to see violent films while they are years younger than the certificate, is misguided, delusional and actually abusive. It shows the same lack of joined-up thinking about the consequences. There is no reason why children would be undisturbed by these games, and deep down they are deeply disturbed.

Other factors like over prescription of drugs and medications that change a child's mood and behaviour do not help either. Diets would be another contributing factor;

brains are never fully satiated because there's no nutritional content in our packaged foods anymore. They are full of not only something that's more addictive than heroin, sugar, but there are so many additives and preservatives that can cause any brain, child or adult to go a bit 'crazy'.

But in our role as parents, we can have positive influence. We are all desperate to get some sleep, yes. But the sleep we lack in the early stages to invest in the relationship with our child may mean our child has all parts of their frontal lobe wired properly. It's the part of the brain that allows them to cope better with stress. As an adult, does that 'baby' have better coping skills and feel a deeper trust to come to you as a teenager with pressures and concerns? I wondered if by helping our babies develop to their full potential, we could be sure we'd done our best not to create a 'rioter' for example — confused, hurt and hurting others. Imagine the sleep that you would lose as that person's mother then? And 'then' may be too late to heal or resolve.

Why Babies Don't Cry in Africa

An African Woman Shares Her Experience

I was born and grew up in Kenya and Cote d'Ivoire. From the age of fifteen I lived in the UK. However, I always knew that I wanted to raise my children (whenever I had them) at home in Kenya. And yes, I assumed I was going to have them. I am a modern African woman, with two university degrees, and a fourth generation working woman — but when it comes to children, I am typically African. The assumption remains that you are not complete without them; children are a blessing which would be crazy to avoid. Actually the question does not even arise.

I started my pregnancy in the UK. The urge to deliver at home was so strong that I sold my practice, set up a new business and moved house and country within five months of finding out I was pregnant. I did what most expectant mothers in the UK do — I read voraciously: Our Babies, Ourselves, Unconditional Parenting, anything by Sears — the list goes on. (My grandmother later commented that babies don't read books and really all I needed to do was 'read' my baby). Everything I read said that African babies cried less than European babies. I was intrigued as to why.

When I went home I observed. I looked out for mothers and babies and they were everywhere, though very young African ones, under six weeks, were mainly at home. The first thing I noticed is that despite their ubiquitousness, it is actually quite difficult to actually 'see' a Kenyan baby. They are usually incredibly well wrapped up before being carried or strapped onto their mother (sometimes father). Even older babies strapped onto a back are further protected from the elements by a large blanket. You would be lucky to catch sight of a limb, never mind an eye or nose. The wrapping is a womb-like replication. The babies are literally cocooned from the stresses of the outside world into which they are entering.

My second observation was a cultural one. In the UK, it was understood that babies cry. In Kenya, it was quite the opposite. The understanding is that babies don't cry. If they do – something is horribly wrong and must be done to rectify it immediately. My English sister-in-law summarised it well. "People here," she said, "really don't like babies crying, do they?"

It all made much more sense when I finally delivered and my grandmother came from the village to visit. As it happened, my baby did cry a fair amount. Exasperated and tired, I forgot everything I had ever read and sometimes joined in the crying too. Yet for my grandmother it was simple, "Nyonyo (breastfeed her)!" It was her answer to every single peep.

There were times when it was a wet nappy, or that I had put her down, or that she needed burping, but mainly she just wanted to be at the breast – it didn't really matter whether she was feeding or just having a comfort moment. I was already wearing her most of the time and co-sleeping with her, so this was a natural extension to what we were doing. I suddenly learned the not-so-difficult secret of the joyful silence of African babies. It was a simple needs-met symbiosis that required a total suspension of ideas of what should be happening and an embracing of what was actually going on in that moment. The bottom line was that my baby fed a lot – far more than I had ever read about and at least five times as much as some of the stricter feeding schedules I had seen.

At about four months, when a lot of urban mothers start to introduce solids as previous guidelines had recommended, my daughter returned to newborn-style hourly breastfeeding, which was a total shock. Over the past four months, the time between feeds had slowly started to increase. I had even started to treat the odd patient without my breasts leaking or my daughter's nanny interrupting the session to let me know my daughter needed a feed.

Most of the mothers in my mother and baby group had duly started to introduce baby rice (to stretch the feeds) and all the professionals involved in our children's lives – pediatricians, even doulas, said that this was ok. Mothers needed rest too, we had done amazingly to get to four months exclusively breastfeeding, and they assured us our babies would be fine. Something didn't ring true for me and even when I tried, half-heartedly, to mix some pawpaw (the traditional weaning food in Kenya) with expressed milk and offer it to my daughter, she was having none of it.

So I called my grandmother. She laughed and asked if I had been reading books again. She carefully explained how breastfeeding was anything but linear. "She'll tell you when she's ready for food – and her body will too."

"What will I do until then?" I was eager to know.

"You do what you did before, regular nyonyo."

So my life slowed down to what felt like a standstill again. While many of my contemporaries marvelled at how their children were sleeping longer now that they had introduced baby rice and were even venturing to other foods, I was waking hourly or every two hours with my daughter and telling patients that the return to work wasn't panning out quite as I had planned.

I soon found that quite unwittingly, I was turning into an informal support service for other urban mothers. My phone number was doing the rounds and many times while I was feeding my baby I would hear myself uttering the words, "Yes, just keep feeding him/her. Yes, even if you have just fed them. Yes, you might not even manage to get out of your pyjamas today. Yes, you still need to eat and drink like a horse. No, now might not be the time to consider going back to work if you can afford not to." And finally, I assured mothers, "It will get easier." I had to just trust this last one as it hadn't gotten easier for me, yet.

A week or so before my daughter turned five months, we travelled to the UK for a wedding and for her to meet family and friends. Because I had very few other demands, I easily kept up her feeding schedule. Despite the disconcerted looks of many strangers as I fed my daughter in many varied public places (most designated breastfeeding rooms were in restrooms which I just could not bring myself to use), we carried on.

At the wedding, the people whose table we sat at noted, "She is such an easy baby – though she does feed a lot." I kept my silence. Another lady commented, "Though I did read somewhere that African babies don't cry much." I could not help but laugh.

My Grandmother's gentle wisdom:

1. Offer the breast every single moment that your baby is upset – even if you have just fed her.
2. Co-sleep. Many times you can feed your baby before they are fully awake, which

> *will allow them to go back to sleep easier and get you more rest.*
> 3. *Always take a flask of warm water to bed with you at night to keep you hydrated and the milk flowing.*
> 4. *Make feeding your priority (especially during growth spurts) and get everyone else around you to do as much as they can for you. There is very little that cannot wait.*
>
> *Read your baby, not the books. Breastfeeding is not linear – it goes up and down and also in circles. You are the expert on your baby's needs.*
>
> www.incultureparent.com[1]
>
> ---
> [1] Robertson J, et al. (1969) "John – 17 months: Nine Days in a Residential Nursery", 16mm film video: The Robertson Centre. Accompanied by a printed "Guide to the Film" Series: British Medical Association / Concord Film Council.

We would often think of the lady that grew up with Warren and his family in Africa, Mavis. We would say to each other: "What would Mavis do?" This became another really good question to ask when we got confused. Because Mavis would wear her babies, sleep with her babies and breastfeed her babies whenever they asked. It was normal and natural for her. It reminded us that maybe what we were doing was not so natural and help us to remember that it was okay to stay attached to Beaudy if that's what he wanted that day, or night. It made him happy and content, and therefore we were too.

Why Babies Don't Cry in the Wild

Now picture this scenario. In hunter/gatherer times, what happened to the babies and how did they parent naturally? It's interesting to know why they too breastfed the babies every time they fussed.

The baby was put on the breast every time they fussed for two reasons: one, for survival, and the second was for instinctive peace and harmony for all involved.

Now, understand the greatness of this concept because it will help you as a mother, especially as a breastfeeding mother, to understand fully the reasons why your emotions are amplified at times and why your hormones play a massive role.

In the wild, if the baby cried it would mean that you and the village were all under threat, because there is greater likelihood that a predator could detect you. So during these times, the baby would quickly latch on to the breast and no sound would be heard.

Of course, we live in the 21st century, in big houses and safe from any predators. We don't need to worry about being hunted down. But our babies don't know this and the way we have been programmed or hardwired hasn't changed. Our DNA is still programmed for survival.

So, here comes the part that makes sense in our day and age and how we live in the Western world. Hormonally we are still connected to the 'flight or fight' response when our babies cry. When our babies cry, we release adrenalin that makes us want to move, do something, and naturally and instinctively calm or pacify them. This is because we are still getting that adrenalin through our bodies that would normally prompt us to protect the baby and ourselves. It's instinctual. The only thing that's different is somewhere along the line, we have been told by books and generations of modern parents that it's okay to let your baby cry to sleep in a bid to get some yourself. We've been fooled into believing that a baby's cry is about trying to control you. The truth will be revealed later on. and let me reassure you that there are other ways of getting sleep without tears.

Now if we do not use up that energy, that adrenalin, it's very easy to have feelings of rage or anger and end up in tears yourself. We are not grabbing our crying babies in the wild and running away from a big lion. We are not using that adrenalin in a flight or fight response to flee and save the family.

The hormones released are being ignored. Baby toocan then release too much adrenalin from their crying. In this situation, the mother can feel helpless, upset or angry for a while. I interviewed Meagan, a mother who exclusively breastfed her son, and here's what she had to say:

> *"I would often find myself with extra energy and running around when my son started showing signs that he was tired or hungry. I would be doing everything I could to facilitate being able to relax and feed him. It was as though I was using my adrenalin and intuition all at the same time, knowing that he was about to start crying if I didn't get his next feed, bath or sleep ready. I realized those feelings of not wanting him to cry were natural and healthy. It made him feel secure and I felt relaxed and calm too, once I began breastfeeding him again."*

There's much to learn from how we respond and what our bodies are doing. It means we can make peace with the desire to help our babies without either parties releasing tears or feeling upset.

I hear from many mums that they feel uncomfortable hearing their baby cry. The only reason we Western women allow it is for the desperate need to have our 'life' back the way it was before, and to feel 'in control'. An addiction to the thought of needing the same sleep as pre-baby can move anyone to try anything. Very few parents are at peace with hearing their baby cry to sleep. It makes me wonder why as a culture we decided it was okay and nobody ever questioned the concept of not picking up a baby if it cried. If you cried I'd cuddle you, so why wouldn't you do it to a baby who feels helpless? It really made me realise it was purely a cultural thing when my brother came here on holiday from Thailand where he has been living for 10 years with his Thai wife. She asked him why there were so many babies being pushed around in prams, crying and ignored. She said babies don't cry in Thailand. I guess it's about a culture not wanting them to cry. I think it's important to ask yourself why you want your baby to cry, and if you conclude that it's not necessary for baby or yourself to be upset or anxious then these tips are going to be of great help to you. There are solutions for sleeping babies minus the crying not just in Africa or Asia; there's a middle ground in Western cultures too!

If you've ever felt anger or an energy that felt angry run through your body like adrenalin when you hear your baby cry then know that this is normal. Some mothers feel that they have to put their crying baby safely in a cot and leave the room so they can regain composure and take some deep breaths before they come back in to settle them.

Because I'm about prevention, not cure, I'd like to think that I'd be attending to my baby's needs before any crying has to occur. Remember, if you keep your baby close, you are in tune with its needs and the baby may not need to cry unless it is sick and something is wrong. I also had some great advice from an ABA counsellor once who told me it was okay to cry in front of my baby. She said crying was a real human emotion and it was important I teach my child that I have real feelings too, and that this may teach him empathy.

Although, if you feel so overwhelmed and have negative thoughts while your baby is crying, it may help to consider that this adrenalin release is natural, and actually what you would normally use to protect your child if you were in the wild. In hunter-gatherer days, babies rarely cried. They kept them close and wore them, so if a baby cried, it meant they were in danger. In our western culture, we don't use that adrenalin and it may get stored in our body creating stress and feelings of rage. It's good to pick your baby up and go for a walk. Change the pace and use the energy; use a breathing rhythm to get you both synchronised again then assess what you need to do. Use your heart, not your head.

Chapter Five

Breastfeeding Bliss

"A baby nursing at a mother's breast ... is an undeniable affirmation of our rootedness in nature."

— David Suzuki

Natural Breastfeeding

In the last 100 years or so, there has been an emotional revolution where women wanted and sought emotional freedom from their children. This attitude brought about the introduction of bottle feeding with other animals' milk. It has actually back-fired because we have made our children more emotionally dependent with more social and emotional challenges by not investing in the first years of our baby's lives by breastfeeding, and having the attachment and parenting style that comes with the act of natural breastfeeding.

It is an act that is sometimes lost in the generations. My mother didn't tell me about this subject but that's because her mother couldn't breastfeed. I later learnt that my grandmother remembers her mother breastfeeding her baby brother in bed, lying down together, and that it was common in their day to breast feed up until the age of around four. The kids would be playing in the park together and she has memories of the children coming up to the parents' laps and having a feed and then going back to play.

In Australia, the statistics of breastfeeding past the age of 6 months old is now only 14%. If people don't see it happen past 6 months of age then few are going to consider it natural or socially acceptable. If women don't see it then they aren't going to be inspired to trial extended breastfeeding.[1]

One of the biggest myths surrounding breastfeeding is that it is purely for food. Since it is so much more and a natural choice, it's easy to see why so many mums are committed to trying it, but then tortured into giving up. The biggest hurdle is the choice we have. If we didn't have a choice would we try to make the breastfeeding work? Would we be more determined? If you knew there was no alternative, would you persist? In this day and age, it's important to know that we have a choice about almost everything in life. We are lucky to be able to live in a society where we are not pressured into unwanted actions. The only reason I'm even bringing up this idea of persisting with something like breastfeeding is because of the deep sadness so many mums share with me when they say they couldn't feed or they had to give up. Nobody should ever have to feel that way, so I want to make sure that if you have all the information and access to help. So if you do choose this natural life experience for you and your family that you get a chance to do it.

My milk didn't come in until Beaudy was 6 days old and I had an army of people around me trying to make this happen. My midwife knew I wanted to feed naturally and after a blissful birth, it felt just as nerve wracking as the days before he was born. Nobody told me it was going to be a journey too. But it was my private midwife, Jan Ireland, who kept a close check on us all. Yes, she milked me like a cow, and yes it hurt, but I was determined to allow this normal and natural process to occur.

For the first few days of Beaudy's life, we were constantly weighing him and he was getting close to dropping too much weight. We all agreed that after giving it a really good go, the next day, which was the fourth day, we would start with some organic goat's milk formula to help him thrive. That night, he fed constantly! I mean without a break, from one side, to the next and then to the next again … over and over. I was so tired, I felt like I was hallucinating, but the whole time I never questioned what was happening; I just had a primal instinct to feed on demand, or as my baby needed. I trusted my baby knew what it was doing and interestingly enough, this scenario created an imprint in my mind to always trust that he knows what he is doing. It was a great life lesson for us. I learnt this lesson early on and carried it with me in case other people's stories made me question that what he was doing was wrong when it came to frequent feeding. (We get to learn a little more about frequency later on.)

It was as though he fed like he knew the formula was coming. When he put on

---

1 https://www.breastfeeding.asn.au/bf-info/general-breastfeeding-information/breastfeeding-rates-australia

weight, we were all so relieved and excited. He did what he needed to do to survive. It was so remarkable because no book or suggestion would have encouraged me to feed non-stop overnight. In fact, I soon realised that I don't control what he wants to do or how much he wants to feed. He does!

After experiencing some initial overwhelming soreness, I recall my midwife saying to me: "Andi, do you know why breastfeeding hurts?" I said, "No?" She replied: "Because you're not meant to do anything but relax!"

It's true. I was such an overachiever, so her lesson was fitting. I was doing too much, so I saw this as a blessing. Jan was in her sixties and very maternal. I never imagined she'd be the type of person to speak badly, let alone cuss or swear. I was finding the initial feeding stage so challenging that I almost wanted to give up, but then I thought it couldn't be as hard as birthing. Everything seemed so much easier once I had experienced birth. Jan told me that these first few sucks were the (here we go - shock, horror!) the "f*ck sucks"! As a new mother being very careful of my new language around children, I exclaimed: "Jan! What do you mean?" She replied in the most matter of fact way, "You say 'f*uck' Andi for the first few sucks to get you through it." I guess Jan always knew how to get me to laugh, which is very important in any trying time.

I later learned that with the help of really good lactation specialists who are gentle in their approach and see breastfeeding as somewhat of a holistic and spiritual experience, it doesn't need to hurt. In fact, it can be very enjoyable for all parties.

Please know that breastfeeding is a gentle and natural experience. No midwife should hurt you and if you feel uncomfortable about the way you are being treated, please exercise your right to express your opinion. Say gently: "Is there another way we can do this where I can help you? I want to feel relaxed." A big part of milk coming through is relaxation.

It's not merely a physical action, and 'milking' or any kind of hurtful tugging does not need to occur. In fact, if anyone, midwife or not, grabs your breast in a way you do not like, it's important for you to let her know that you don't like it. Lactation Consultant Pinky McKay says that a baby can find its way to your breast and you can assist it with latching and attaching.

In hindsight, it didn't matter anymore, because after being threatened with formula supplementation and monitoring my baby's weight with a safe drop, which was healthy and considered normal after birth, it rained, and then it finally poured.

It was important to me to give my baby my milk. Giving another animal's milk designed for that animal at infancy didn't seem right. It would only be an option for me as a last resort, and it needed to be exactly that: last. On that fifth night Beaudy fed all night without a break, and I only got 15 minutes sleep with him at 6am, just before his weigh in. It was so miraculous that he put on 300grams. And the milk bar was finally open!

I have this theory that if we trust babies know what they are doing in the first six weeks and so we are therefore told to 'demand' feed them, then why don't we trust that they are acting primally and still know what they are doing throughout their entire infancy? I started to look into how this could be our foundation for gentle parenting for life. If we trust that colostrum is not just food, but provides antibodies and immune cells as well as many other vital nutrients our baby needs then why have we forgotten that breast milk too is not just food? If we remember that then maybe we would feed when baby needs and if we trust baby will tell us when it wants to feed then we don't need clocks, books, timers or people to tell us how to parent. We would be more in touch with our intuition and form a strong bond with our baby as we get to know each other.

To bring my milk in, we needed to stimulate the supply so that we could create the milk he needed. There are other ways of stimulating supply that are not physical. I learnt through these experts that these are probably the most important.

It's important to –

- Keep your baby close to you and allow them to feed as often as they desire. However, some babies may be drowsy from a drug you may have had at birth like pethidine or an epidural so you may need to try harder to encourage them to feed. Keeping your baby close ensures synchronicity of hormones and maximum sucking. Their saliva has something in it that stimulates 'let down', so no matter how much you express, your baby's suck will always be more effective.
- Relax. Each mother's breast milk is perfect for her baby. Relaxing so your body can produce prolactin to make breast milk is important. Try relaxing your shoulders after a warm bath before you know you're about to breastfeed. Take a sip of water and as you swallow and exhale, you can relax and exhale which will help a 'let down' response too. You may even like to try having a bath together. It's very common for babies to enjoy a breastfeed while you're in the bath together. The warmth of the water emulates the womb and skin-to-skin contact is very immune boosting.
- Always try to have lots of skin-to-skin contact with your baby, as it can help supply.

Benefits of Breastfeeding

The obvious benefits of breastfeeding are:

- Physical – it's the bonding and touch that is a natural life experience for all. Much research points to the nutritional health benefits, like reduced risks in cancer — not just for baby but for the mother too.
- Emotional – the act of sitting down to breastfeed several times a day means both you and the baby get to relax, and refuel emotionally.
- Financial – it doesn't cost a cent to breastfeed! You save money of formula, bottles and cleaning and sterilisation
- Time – you save so much time having to wash, prepare and check temperature on a bottle
- Development – much research points to how excellent breastfeeding is for speech development as well as boosting immunity
- Solids Preparation – consuming breast milk as a baby prepares one for the variety of foods. They get a taste of it through their mother's milk and the food she consumes. It makes it much easier for the parents to then introduce a variety of solids as the taste is familiar. If there is a certain food that your baby reacts to, or is having a hard time digesting and suffers constipation, this is where extended, full term breastfeeding is wonderful. Your breastmilk will help as you offer a feed after solids to help digest the new food. Your milk will create natural laxatives and enzymes, should your baby require this.

The breasts are positioned by the heart which is where the most amount of blood is, providing warmth. All of babies needs are met in mum's arms, food, hydration, comfort, warmth and entertainment by breastfeeding. If we don't breastfeed, then we have to find other ways to be close and get those needs met.

Understanding Breastfeeding from the Baby's Perspective

On Children
Kahlil Gibran

Your children are not your children.
They are the sons and daughters of Life's longing for itself.
They come through you but not from you,
And though they are with you yet they belong not to you.

You may give them your love but not your thoughts,
For they have their own thoughts.
You may house their bodies but not their souls,
For their souls dwell in the house of tomorrow,
which you cannot visit, not even in your dreams.
You may strive to be like them,
but seek not to make them like you.
For life goes not backward nor tarries with yesterday.

Who is in control?

Many parents like to think they can control or measure and even time breast feeds. This doesn't work because it's a bottle-fed strategy.

Your baby controls your supply. Frequent feeding is healthy and normal. He may actually be stimulating the supply with frequent feeds; some short, some long, some to quench the thirst, some to pacify from a bad dream, some to regulate body temperature. Some feeds are because he craves closeness because maybe we aren't meant to sleep separately. Maybe we are meant to be close just like in the animal kingdom. Maybe the Africans and Asians have it right and us Western women are doing it all wrong and being too detached. Maybe he feeds frequently because he likes to suck. Babies have a very strong desire, and need, to suck. Research shows that this sucking action increases their speech development and even tires them out, putting them into a deeper sleep. There's even something called 'cluster feeding' that babies do before they have a longer stretch of sleep. It's as though they are stocking up for the famine that lies ahead!

Whatever the reason to feed, it isn't always about food and this is why the health benefits of breastfeeding are not limited to nutrition. Hello? Light bulb moment? What if breastfeeding isn't just about feeding? What if we called it breast rearing?

What if we surrender to the notion that your baby knows what he is doing on a primal level? So from the baby's perspective, you're a team. His needs control your supply. Your little person loves you so much, needs you and relies on you. Think of your baby's actions as directing you, and you are just following.

Why is breastfeeding so frequent?

There are a countless reasons why you may breastfeed frequently, especially if you remember that breastfeeding isn't just food. Paediatrician Dr Sears puts it quite simply: because we are designed this way. It's important to know that one of the reasons we may be designed to feed frequently is because breast milk is highly digestible. The milk moves through a tiny baby's digestive system at a rapid rate so their nerve systems can fully develop.

Another animal's formula or milk, which is made for that animal, is not so easy to digest. The protein in cow's milk, for example, (Casein) is too big for the human gut to digest. We therefore can become intolerant to it, forming a mucous or phlegm to coat it and bring it back out through an orifice. In a baby's developing digestive system, the other animal's milk can be so hard to digest that it pretty much 'knocks them out' as the digestive system has to work overtime and gives the nervous system less of a chance to develop at an optimal level.

At about six weeks old, the baby experiences a growth spurt. It's not just physical, but also developmental. Eyesight is starting to improve and as they take in the world around them, it can be quite scary. They will want to be close and it's normal to want to breastfeed non-stop. It may feel like sometimes you just cannot put them down. During this time and any 'growth spurt' time, it's important to remember just how much your baby loves you. They won't be little like this forever; it's just a phase and this phase will pass. Just enjoy holding them for as long as they need if you can and you are not working. Another option is to wear a sling and breastfeed them while they are in the sling so that your hands may be free if needed.

Possible Frequent Reasons for Breastfeeding

- Stimulation of supply: Forcing you to sit and/or lie and rest or fall asleep with them. Forcing you to rest means you will make prolactin, which helps them fall into a deeper sleep. It also allows you to heal and recover from birth or be ready to help them resettle when they need you.

- During a developmental growth spurt, babies may feed frequently to get away from the rest of the world. They may be tired of being passed around from family member to family member or strangers and strange smells. They seek security in your arms and breast.
- Hunger. Tiny stomachs need frequent refilling and feeding is tiring.
- Overtired. It's very easy for a baby to fall asleep on the breast. So try to allow yourself to be in a position where you can stay holding or sleeping with them. This may mean preparing a glass of water to be next to you and snacks like banana or nuts so you don't need to move.

All the above reasons are very normal. Babies do not use you as a dummy or pacifier. Surrender to the frequent feeding and enjoy them. Your baby is a gift.

Comparing human milk to that of animals

Our brains are very similar to that of a monkey. Human milk is designed like monkey's milk — very low in fat. The ratio of whey proteins to casein is similar in both milks (approximately 60/40[2]). The low fat content means that we need to feed more frequently as it passes more frequently through our digestive system. We are designed this way so that we can conserve energy to allow the rest of our brain to develop and stay alert in the wild. Therefore we are designed to always be within arm's reach of our mother for survival. Over the centuries, our lifestyle may have changed but the way our brains and bodies are designed have not. Therefore, to be further from our young defies what we are programmed to do and will feel unnatural. A calling or crying out will happen to ensure you are brought back together. The only animal that has a high fat content in milk is a deer. Their offspring drink the mother's very high fat milk and this allows them to be away from their mother for longer periods of time.

So when a new mum I knew was so exhausted from breast feeding all night and wanted to control or 'comfort cry' and leave her baby cry so she could sleep, I remember my heart being sore thinking about him being distraught and wanting her. In this hospital they gave her sleep medication so that she would sleep and not hear the cries of her baby and said they would 'comfort settle' him in another room. She said she refused the medication on the second night because she said it gave her a headache. It worried me that her body was designed to respond to her baby's cries and the

---

[2] PubMed Comp Biochem Physiol Comp Physiol. 1993 Apr;104(4):793-7.

medication switched off her senses. She was told by 'health professionals' that this was okay. Some say your baby manipulates you to get what it wants! Is that so? Naughty baby for wanting to be close to you because you are just so divine!

My friend was obviously just exhausted and wasn't functioning and really needed sleep. The best thing to do here is get a full night's sleep by sleeping with your baby. After all it's amazing what you can do once you get some sleep, but at least it isn't traumatic for both parties. But you and your partner need to be aware of why babies wake for you to be comfortable to do so and feel supported in your decision. After all, we are the only mammals that don't keep our young close.

Western women have had all sorts of modern myths passed down to us through the generations. It has become our culture to 'detach' a little too early and have our 'life back' or 'body back'. It may also be for financial reasons and since mothers work too, we don't always have the security of keeping our job when we are out of it for some time. These factors make it hard for us to parent naturally and ease into this life-long relationship and 'job' of nurturing.

In *The Science of Parenting* by Margot Sunderland, she explores the idea that because Western women need to operate heavy machinery such as drive cars and have part time jobs, they require a certain level of concentration and alertness. It would be dangerous to drive a car while sleep-deprived and bleary eyed. If we were in a village community, we would probably walk everywhere and have less responsibility when it came to these sorts of things. However, we have adapted our lifestyle and the way we parent to fit in with our modern world needs even though it may not be natural to do so. Unless you have the right family and community support, children have to deal with parenting like being left to cry to sleep at night. Parenting is a 24-7 job and it's a job that doesn't stop when it gets dark.

A recent study showed that just over 30 per cent of the almost 500 mums surveyed admit to medicating their children to make them sleep or calm them down.[3]

This alarming information highlights how important it is to support mums and their lack of sleep. Not only is it not natural to take a drug or give it to your child, and I understand the importance of life-saving medication in circumstances like emergency but it also doesn't respect nor understand a child's sleep cycle. Next time you come into contact with a new mother, find out what you can do to be of support to her and the whole family.

Another common problem is new mothers taking medication for postnatal depression, which stems from sleep deprivation.

---

3 http://www.heraldsun.com.au/news/national/australian-mums-prefer-sleep-to-sex-and-many-want-weight-loss-ahead-of-smarter-kids/story-e6frf7l6-1226139354441

It does take courage to speak about depression and medication. It's to be admired because being 'depressed' is frowned upon and it shouldn't be. Courage is about having heart. In fact the word itself comes from a French word, le cœur, meaning heart, so to.

Some governments are already seeing the importance of supporting new mothers. That's why legislation of parental leave is really important. It probably should be twelve months of paid parental leave like in Norway and other countries. If the government injected money into the parental leave system, they may actually be providing a solution to a much larger health care issue. The natural wellness approach is to not wait until the mother is not coping.

One day in chiropractic practice, my husband consoled a first-time mum who was beside herself. Her doctor, a paediatrician, had told her to only feed her baby every four hours so she could get some sleep. She had brought her baby in for a consultation and chiropractic check-up because her baby was constantly crying. When she shared this information, my husband had to explain that not only was it wrong, but that her instinct that told her it was wrong, was right! Needless to say she had developed mastitis and was at risk of losing her milk. Following her instinct to feed when the baby asked meant for a happy baby and mother. The challenge was to explain to her that there were other ways of getting sleep without tears.

What if breast milk isn't food?

The truth is that the breast meets every need a newborn has except a dirty nappy. With skin-to-skin contact regulating their temperature and other vital neurological developments, the baby does not have to expend the energy they would have to if they were doing it themselves. Milk is a live substance and produces prolactin which is a vital property that helps induce sleep, while the act of feeding releases hormones to relax both mum and baby. This makes it all the more appropriate to feed your new baby to sleep a few times a night. If baby is hungry or thirsty the breast milk nourishes, and it provides the ultimate security for a newborn, whose brain has only developed 25% at birth. He behaves only on a primal level. Breastfeeding is also recognised as pain-relieving, and in the early days has more antibodies than blood. This is why the most natural way to help your baby through a tough teething time is to breastfeed him back to sleep. If baby is feeling under the weather, he often turns to the breast, and with good reason. The germ is passed to mum, she makes relevant antibodies, and then passes them back to baby at subsequent feeds.

You could perceive it as a baby's first "vaccination" and the most nutritionally complete food they will ever consume.

CHAPTER FIVE - BREASTFEEDING BLISS

The most natural way for you and your baby to fall asleep is by breastfeeding. There's never any need for tears or tantrums because you have everything you need to settle your baby with breast-reared baby. Not only are we hardwired to do it but there are so many benefits besides sleeping that it could be a book in itself!

Now, not all women are able to breastfeed and no woman should ever have to feel bad for not doing so;. although each and every woman shouldn't give up trying without a damn good fight. You really need not only the right support and help, but also the right information. Breastfeeding satisfies all your baby's needs. It's nutritionally, emotionally, psychologically and financially beneficial for everyone.

All your baby's needs are met in the arms of the mother as he breastfeeds: temperature regulation, nutrition, immune cells, antibodies, hydration, entertainment, trust, psychological and analgesic properties for teething, and there's even financial benefits!

Some may say with sadness that they didn't have milk and had to turn to the bottle. Most didn't have the help of a good lactation specialist or associations such as the Australian Breastfeeding Association. If you're pregnant and thinking about breastfeeding, or wanting to try it for your next child, please get in touch with these people. There are too many books and 'old school' doctors who give advice about breastfeeding as though it were merely a mechanistic activity. It's actually quite spiritual. By that I mean it's something that is very intuitive and can be meditative for the mother and baby. It's important to demand feed. When people now ask me how often I fed my baby, I reply, "Whenever he asked". Every time the baby fusses, if you put him on the breast, you are sure to keep your supply up. Milk will only dry up if you listen to old-fashioned advice like "feed every two hours or every four hours", and "Don't feed again. They're full. You'll overfeed." Some of the myths and misconceptions are outrageous. First of all, you can't over feed a breastfed baby. Women who watch the clock and not their baby, end up not being able to make milk, or get their milk to come through. Others end up with oversupply and mastitis or blocked milk ducts, which became very dangerous. This was me.

So next time you are watching a puppy snuggle into its mother, watch and see if the mother looks at the clock before she offers the litter the next feed, and take this relaxed, go-with-the-flow approach on board. You'll be surprised how enjoyable it is to be in that moment, even if it is for a short period of time.

Breastfeeding Myths

MYTH
You'll over feed your baby

TRUTH
You can't over feed a breastfed baby. The beauty of breast feeding is that your baby controls how much milk they need for that feed and day. They also control what type of milk they need each time. For example, they may need foremilk (watery type milk) to quench their thirst, hind milk (fatty milk, which is rich in essential fatty acids to put them into a deeper sleep or put on weight in anticipation for when they crawl or walk), or milk rich in antibodies or immune cells because they are fighting infection that day. You make the exact milk they need and you never have to worry about measuring, weighing, heating or sterilising. Your baby will control the amount of calories it needs. This is particularly good when you have started introducing solids (from 6 months on). You needn't worry about a varied diet right away; take your time to introduce one food at a time, slowly. Your breast milk will fill in the gaps, supplying what your baby missed out on and needs, like extra protein. It's truly incredible. Research shows breastfed babies have less chance of ever being overweight later in life.

MYTH
Your baby will rely on your breast to fall asleep

TRUTH
Your breast is the most natural way a baby knows how to fall asleep. It's more natural than a bit of plastic on the end of a pacifier and when they do fall asleep on the breast, it's usually age appropriate. Eventually, as your baby gets older, explores more of the world around them and feels safe in your care, he will also want to fall asleep other ways too. From six to eight months onwards when your baby is exploring other foods, the type of milk you produce will change, but the foods aren't always rich in all the nutrition your baby needs. So they may need to consume milk you make that makes up for that, depending on what they ate that day. At this age, not one food group can solely provide all the nutrition your baby needs the way your milk can. Hence your breastfeeds should still be very frequent and when your baby asks. So when they do choose to fall asleep on the breast, they are usually extracting hind milk to put them, and you, into a deep sleep.

This is the bonus for you — that breastfeeding makes you tired. A common misunderstanding is that breastfeeding makes you tired because mothers fall asleep doing it, but in fact it is the hormones that are released that ensure a mother gets enough rest. The problem is actually the solution.

Enjoy the deep sleep you both get. Try to feed your baby and go straight to sleep too. It's a beautifully natural way for you both to get some sleep.

MYTH
Your baby is using you as a pacifier

TRUTH

I've heard so many mothers say they feel their baby is just pacifying on them. I felt this way too at times but always remind myself that they may just be getting the hind milk or immune cells and are tired; they will fall asleep only to wake minutes later, have a few sucks and are 'out for the count'. When my baby reached the age of 12 months, he preferred being rocked to sleep if he didn't fall asleep on the breast. His stomach may have been full from the dinner I gave him an hour before. I would look down at him when I felt like he had enough and asked if he wanted "bouncy bouncy"? He would remove himself and sit up. I'd then rock him to sleep on a fit ball we had in our room. Only a mother knows their child and what they need, when they need it. But know that your baby is not 'using' you and it's always nicer to be gentle and ask them if they've had enough. The best advice I ever got was from a man who had six children and his had wife breastfed all six! He told me never to detach my baby from the breast. He said they will tell *you* when they've had enough. I learned to trust my baby and be more at peace with the whole: "They're in control, not always me."

Breastfeeding is great for sleep because of the consistency of the milk that you produce for your baby. Besides the fact that cow's milk is made for cows, goat milk for goats and human milk is designed for humans, it's exactly what your baby needs for that day at that time. Your body takes care of the fat to water ratio and which antibodies or immune cells your baby needs. You don't ever have to think about it. The protein in human milk is just the right size for a baby human. Cow's milk protein, casein, is too large for the human gut to easily digest and your tiny baby's developing digestive system may not cope with the challenge.

The fatty part of breast milk, hind milk, is rich in Essential Fatty Acids (EFAs), which put your baby into a deeper sleep. It's very common for a baby to want to feed even twenty minutes after they've fed for a 'top-up' to get this fatty milk, or 'cluster feed', and eventually fall into a deep sleep, which is why it's imperative to watch your baby and not the clock when feeding.

The sucking action is also very different to that of a bottle. Babies store the breast milk in their cheeks and control the amount they swallow. To extract the milk is much harder than from a bottle and our bodies are designed this way on purpose to tire the baby. It's said this sucking action is also great for speech development in many research articles too. You also minimise the chances of your baby getting colic or reflux because they control the right amount and flow.

MYTH
Pull the baby off the breast when he's finished

TRUTH

I found that the best advice I got from a chiropractor whose wife breastfed their seven children was to do the exact opposite. He approached me at a seminar and said, "Never detach the baby from the feed/breastfeed. They will decide when they've had enough and remove themselves". This was really interesting because it instilled in me that I should trust my baby. It was so beneficial because babies can have a little break in between because they can get tired. It may appear that they have stopped sucking or are finished, but they may be having a rest and then working up to get to the hind milk so they can fall into a deeper sleep.

MYTH
I ran out of breast milk; I dried up

TRUTH

While this can actually happen, lots of mothers may mistake not getting a 'let down' for drying up. There are tiny blood capillaries in your breasts that can shrink when you are stressed. When these shrink, it can stop your milk coming out. As long as your baby demands milk, you will have a supply. In the beginning, you can have an over-supply and engorgement in your breasts. Your baby will then work out exactly how much it needs. Your breasts then feel less engorged, but you may mistake this feeling for drying up. But milk is always there; it's the let-down that may take some time. Try to choose a quiet spot for you and your baby to feed and have a bottle or glass of water handy, take a sip of water and exhale. Milk can usually flow once you relax and swallow the water. Be patient. Your baby is drawing it out.

> **Don't mistake drying up for:**
> - Not getting a let-down straight away
> - No longer having engorgement
> - Not seeing much milk in your expressed bottle. Your baby is always much more efficient at drawing milk out then you can ever be by express pumping. This is not only because of their strong sucking action but also because they have an enzyme in their saliva that stimulates a let-down reflex.
>
> **Avoid drying up by:**
> - Refusing feeding on a 'routine'. If you are not feeding often enough, you may not produce prolactin and you may also not stimulate supply.
> - Stay relaxed. One way you can do this is by feeding.
> - Feed as often as possible in the first couple of months of your baby's life. These months will establish your supply for the future.

Helpful Hormones

By breastfeeding your baby, you will receive oxytocin, the love hormone that helps you to feel relaxed and fall asleep easily. Often the mum will fall asleep with the baby at the same time and this hormone only leaves the body after around 10 minutes. Imagine having to get up to turn on lights in the kitchen, leave your baby to cry in the dark room while you wash a bottle, heat the milk, check the temperature, wake up too much from the lights and activity, go into the room to a baby that's no longer half asleep, feed them and then have to resettle the baby and yourself. No lights or crying are necessary with breastfeeding as you can get to the baby as it stirs. Many mums have said they have experienced waking just seconds or minutes before the baby and not known why they were awake, only to realise the baby has woken for a feed. Your hormones are synchronised and you wake at the same time, which means if your husband or partner chooses to sleep in the same room as you, you can all be together without them waking.

Another helpful hormone is Cholecystokinin (CCK), which is released if you and baby lie down while you're feeding. Both mum and baby can fall asleep together and this CCK is what puts both parties into a very deep sleep. Sometimes 40 minutes will feel like four hours. It's truly miraculous.

Despite what most say, everyone can breastfeed with the right help, unless there's something physiologically wrong with you, like inverted nipples. Even if your baby has a cleft palette and attachment is a challenge, it's still possible with the right help from a great lactation consultant and information from the Australian Breastfeeding Association.

If you're pregnant or have begun breastfeeding, join the Australian Breastfeeding Association or at least do research on their website and read all the articles to get the help and support you'll need. The website has information on feeding issues, settling tips, sleep research, dealing with unwanted criticism and how to express if you must return to work. Their 1800 mum to mum help line saved me many a time and the counsellors are trained, experienced breastfeeding mums.

I know lots of mums whose milk 'dried up' because they didn't feed when the baby asked; especially in my mum's generation when they were told to feed every four hours. I would sometimes feed every 20-40 minutes to establish my supply and then continue to stimulate my supply depending on what was happening in my life and what stresses were around.

But as time progressed, my baby became more efficient and the feeds were less frequent as we slowly introduced solids.

The World Health Organization states that we should keep breastfeeding babies until they are two and beyond. Up until this age, the main source of nutrition will come from milk. That's human milk and not solids.

Some would challenge me and say that once my baby had teeth, there is no need for breastfeeding and put him onthe bottle. Great question, so I researched that too. First of all, it's not 'strange' or 'wrong' to continue breastfeeding once your baby has teeth. In fact it's so natural to continue breastfeeding it's not funny, especially if you remember breastmilk is not just food, but is the main source of nutrition. If you must go to work, around this time, there are ways in which you may like to continue breastfeeding by expressing your milk into a bottle or bringing your baby to work with you for feeds if at all possible with a nanny. It just may be more beneficial than introducing a formula too soon. You see the calcium in cow's milk is made for cows and the nutrition in goat's milk is designed for goats. We wrote about this in our book *7 Things Your Doctor Forgot to Tell You*. Human milk is designed for humans. We cannot assimilate the calcium nor digest the protein that's in cow's milk, so our human milk is just perfect. If we don't have all our teeth yet, isn't that one sign that we aren't ready for a diet exclusively made up of solids? We are the only species that continue to drink milk after infancy and to do it from another animal just doesn't make sense to me.

CHAPTER FIVE - BREASTFEEDING BLISS

In the beginning, you may have difficulties with breastfeeding, such as milk coming through, or it may be painful if attachment isn't correct. There are a number of challenges you may face, but rest assured, there is help around and any mum who really wants to lactate, can. There are wonderful breastfeeding counsellors and support groups around to help you.

Later on, when your baby is older, it may be too hard to find the quiet time you need to relax, bond and feed as you may have other children or commitments. I was in the park one day with my baby boy when he was 13 months old. A woman with her baby was playing with us on the same see-saw and she asked how old Beaudy was and was envious I was still feeding. She said she fed her first two until they didn't want it anymore but felt that nobody gave her the support she needed to continue with the third child and she gave up reluctantly after four months. As a mother of only one, I asked her why. I didn't understand what else you needed and was eager to learn. She explained that when life got busier with two other children, she found it hard to have quiet time to sit down without distraction and feed. I tried to imagine how much easier it would have been with a bottle of formula. Then I ran into a mother of two at my husband's clinic who showed me a way to make it work if you wanted to continue breastfeeding. She said she had a basket of breastfeeding toys. It was a basket of different toys to the ones the toddler was used to playing with and he was only allowed to play with those toys every time she fed the newborn.

Those who feel they need to give up; I will not argue with you. You have to do what's right for you and your family. It's just important to know that there's always a way to make things work, if you want it to, and that there is help from other mothers via the ABA 1800 mum to mum help line. Know that however hard breastfeeding may be, it's also extremely easy. I can't imagine how hard it must be; having to get up to a sick child several times at night and finding medication in the dark, let alone deal with the side effects of it. What could be more easy and natural than breastfeeding your angel back to sleep with the immune cells and analgesic properties your milk provides, without turning on lights or doing very much at all? However, if you feed every time your baby asks, you increase the immunity and may find that your child is never sick compared to his formula-fed friends.

The best thing about breastfeeding is that it truly is a forced way of making sure you are having ample rest and relaxation throughout the day. It's your baby's way of making sure you are looking after you so you can look after them. You really are a team! If your baby is asking for frequent feeding, besides looking at all the reasons they may require it, have a look at why perhaps you may need it too! It's a healthy way to be.

Chapter Six

Where's the Village

"The largest percentage of insecure infants are found in cultures that require the earliest self-reliance."

— Sharon Heller

Getting To Know Your Baby

In the Western world, our mothers don't always live in the same house with us like in other communities around the world and sometimes they don't even live in the same country. With little family around, how do we get to know our little person when as soon as it's born it's passed around like a football to excited loved ones and friends or put straight into a cot or another room? If it was a traumatic birth, it may take a little longer as you may have been separated for some time and have a little extra work ahead for the two of you.

I have this thought that our babies don't know they are no longer attached, no longer getting all its needs met via the umbilical cord on tap, without having to ask for or even cry. Other mums have told me they feel it takes around nine months for the baby to realise they are separate. This is interesting because it's at this age that people talk of 'separation anxiety'. It's also around the time that it takes to make a baby, so it seems balanced that if your baby is in you for nine months, it may also take nine months to become aware, and get used to the fact, that you are now two.

With this in mind, if we keep them close, the benefits are that we get to know and understand their own language. We can learn through little signs that they are wanting to feed, needing to be held to regulate body temperature that emulates the womb's 37 degrees womb and maybe even need to be held to push out a fart! Don't they always want to be held and what's wrong with that? The most ridiculous myth I have heard is that "you will spoil your baby by holding them too much". I've never seen a spoilt baby from too much love. And I'm sure they won't always want to be held! Maybe by their girlfriend at 16, but it certainly won't be you while they sleep, so why not enjoy all the cuddles they require now?

If you are beginning to learn that you will be pretty much tied up holding your baby for a big chunk of your day while they're in infancy, then how on earth, I hear you thinking, do we get anything done? This is where baby-wearing is 'king' and a 'village' comes into play.

Life in the African village where my husband worked as a paramedic in Johannesburg was interesting. He said some mothers in Africa didn't put nappies on their child. Warren asked them, "But what if your baby needs to do a poo? How do you know when they're about to do that?" The women replied, "How would you not know?" Only now that we have been wearing our baby as they do, and keeping it close, have we seen what they mean. We could sometimes tell when our son is about to push or pass a bowel movement. He wore nappies but we felt there was much more about the baby-wearing that we were still to learn from these women in the village. It was their natural way of parenting that inspired us to become more in tune with our baby's needs.

The 'Village' Concept

The old saying; "It takes a village to raise a child" became our mantra. If we were going to parent this way, that is 'naturally', then we needed help. We didn't have the luxury of having family close by. They lived in other states and countries and had busy lives. But we did have short term, loving enthusiastic help and visitations from the grandparents. It didn't last forever, but it felt like we needed them.

It felt strange that we all lived in houses far away from each other when we could have done with loving nurturers close by, just like in a village. In Western society we live in big houses, alone and far away from families. In African or Asian villages, they live in close communities and are there to help 24-7. They allow the new mother to rest and bond with the baby. She wears the baby, sleeps with the baby and keeps the baby close to get to know its needs.

Once you have birthed, your body will take time to recover, even if it is a natural birth. You have just run a marathon and possibly had some sort of medication or operation and so your body is going to have to process all of that too. It is you that may need to be mothered and nurtured first so that you can heal and then feel like

CHAPTER SIX - WHERE'S THE VILLAGE

doing some mothering yourself. Your baby will require you close 24-7. You won't have time to do the usual domestic duties. It's really important to have help around and remember this phase is just that; a phase. It will pass.

I was starting to understand this concept and missed my 'village'. It made me wonder why we didn't have that kind of support. I'd be pushing the pram and would dream about a life where my neighbours were my family. We'd sit under a tree and feed together and maybe sleep a bit. Instead there's pressure on the new mum to have it all under control in such a short time. Let's not forget to mention we are expected to have our pre-baby body back too soon too! Eventually, I created my own village. Next time the neighbour offered to play with my son for an hour, when I knew he wanted extra interaction, I accepted. When I broke my arm and couldn't brush my hair, I allowed my neighbour to tie it in a ponytail for me. It's a shame I had to wait Until I broke my arm and became totally dependent before I accepted help. You don't have to feel like you have it under control, and everybody loves to help a new mother and baby.

There was a documentary we watched where the documentary makers showed Nigerian mothers 'Western world dads' who were wearing the baby in a sling or carrier. The women looked confused and laughed at the dads and asked why they were wearing the babies. My husband asked me why the woman would think this because he was wearing our baby all the time to establish a bond, especially because I was creating a natural bond through breastfeeding. We concluded it was because the mum naturally bonds with the baby by wearing it because she has a part of anatomy that they don't have that satisfies all the baby's needs — the breasts. It was important to keep baby close so it could have access to this life support or supply at any time. Fathers in Africa would probably be out working in the fields and the mothers would have stayed home to be the home maker. Now this is very hard to do because most of us 'women' are working now and we love to work or want to work. Some are single mothers and have to work. It makes things like government or employee paid parental leave really important if we want to be able to gently raise a society of attached parents and children. Being home for the first six to twelve months would set up a great foundation for both baby and parent. But we have adapted the concept to suit our Western world needs, so that fathers wearing their babies sometimes too, creating a loving bond between Father and baby, and giving the Mother a chance to do something else, which is usually sleep.

How to create a 'village' for your baby

I was lucky enough to have come into contact with some remarkable people and associations during my first tough year or so. I was an active member of The Australian Breastfeeding Association and I got in touch with them to offer my personal story to hopefully inspire other mums who may not have the confidence to give breastfeeding a try.

Here is the article that was published in May 2012. It went with a lovely cover I shot with my son. The photographer, mother Vicky Leon, also donated her time.

The ABA is My Village

*Before Andi Lew became a mum in January 2010, she thought breastfeeding was "mainly food", but through her son, Beaudy Shae, she discovered "it's so much more". The TV presenter (*Shopping for Love*), radio announcer (3AW's wellness reporter), co-author (7 Things Your Doctor Forgot To Tell You) and chiropractic assistant shares her breastfeeding journey—how she learnt to trust her body to produce what her baby needed, gained confidence to feed in public, and savoured empathetic words from ABA counsellors when times got tough.*

I was someone who didn't know if I could breastfeed at all, as my milk only came in on day six. The fifth night was scary with the ultimatum that if it didn't come through, we were going to have to supplement with formula. I think my baby must have known, don't they always? He was just as determined as me. He fed that night non-stop. I swapped sides without a break until 6am—two hours before his weigh-in—I finally got 15 minutes sleep. He was determined to get that milk through, and then it rained and poured!

I used to be the kind of person that would hold a cloth, wrap or scarf over him in public or even at home for fear someone may see and until I saw a Facebook group called "*If you have a problem with my breastfeeding, put a blanket over your head.*" I thought it was hilarious and it was a turning point for me. Why should we have to hide something we are hardwired to do? Then a religious Dutch patient of my chiropractic husband's [Warren Sipser] asked in his thick accent: "Are you doing bottle or natural?" It made me realise how unnatural a bottle was. (something about how it wasn't "bottle or breast?")

There's so much unwanted criticism, about feeding in public, about what age it's appropriate to continue and frequency. Some myths and misconceptions I used to have is that breastfeeding is food but I've now researched this and it's so much more. It's immune cells, hydration, antibodies, temperature regulation, great for speech development and nutrition that no other food group can replicate. It's amazing how intelligent the body is that the baby can extract and make the exact type of milk it needs that day depending on what germs or virus it may have come into contact with or how constipated or thirsty or hungry the baby is It still blows my mind how your baby controls what type of calories it needs by extracting either foremilk or hindmilk so the mother doesn't have to worry about volume if she feeds whenever the baby asks.

People who offered advice about frequency would say to watch the clock, not my baby. "Feed every 4 hours", or "He just had solids, why are you feeding again?" "Give water not milk." How did I know if my baby needed immune cells that day? I didn't. The comments really confused me. The advice came from people who didn't breastfeed or had breastfed but were given advice by people in their day who didn't understand. As a result, I ended up with mastitis that left me so sick and bedridden because I didn't feed when my baby asked. I used to cry thinking that the only way my baby would fall asleep was on the breast and that he'd be doing that until he was 4! I later learned it was age appropriate when he does and he eventually fell asleep other ways too. I soon learned about the supply and demand rule- I don't control what my baby needs, my baby does. I surrendered to that after speaking with some ABA counsellors and read books by Pinky McKay, who all encouraged me to trust my instincts and my baby's cues. Pinky became a friend as we did a book swap, and she gave me confidence to follow my heart as I didn't believe in control crying and that his frequent feeding was normal. Beaudy's tiny stomach could only handle a small amount at a time and boy was he growing at a rapid rate!

The people around me with unwanted criticism did mean well. They were in a desperate bid to help me get sleep. This sleep deprivation issue is a whole new world! There's a massive market of people helping mums get sleep. I discovered that breastfeeding is truly the most natural way of allowing mother and baby fall into a deep, quality sleep. Thank God for the oxytocin and CCK (cholecystokinin) hormones! I could never imagine having to get up, turn on lights, prepare bottles, wait for the right temperature and then walk back upstairs to a crying baby that had been waiting all that time to feed and then settle. Waking right before my baby cries–which always makes me feel we are so spiritually connected—is easy as I get to him before he wakes up too much and we can both fall back to sleep together without turning on any lights or making noise so that Warren can be in the same room as us.

Warren, who is South African, and I would look to the African cultures and ask: "What would they do in Africa or Asia?" This mantra started when we found ourselves at our birth centre/hospital pre-natal class. We sat in a sterile room watching a "how to breastfeed" DVD. It was quite sad that we needed one to learn something that we are all programmed to innately do! Did my baby need to watch a DVD? No, he knew what to do as he followed the linea alba up to my target areola and suckled! Does an animal in the wild need a DVD? No. In Africa, women would've grown up all sitting under a tree with their aunties and mums and sisters, chatting and watching. It would be a natural subconscious learning. I bet the animal kingdom didn't lie around saying to each other: "Has it been four hours yet?"

As Beaudy got older, some would challenge me and ask if once he had teeth, would I stop breastfeeding? I researched that too. First of all, it's not strange or wrong. In fact it's so natural to continue breastfeeding it just made sense. You see the calcium in cow's milk is made for cows and the nutrition in goat's milk is designed for goats. Warren and I wrote about this in our book—*7 Things Your Doctor Forgot to Tell You*. Human milk is designed for humans! We cannot assimilate the calcium nor digest the protein called casein that's in cow's milk so our human milk is just perfect. If we don't have all our teeth yet, isn't that one sign that we aren't ready for a diet exclusively solids? We are the only species that continues to drink milk after infancy why do it from another animal?

The Australian Breastfeeding Association has been a real lifesaver for me. I found out about it through ABA counsellor and ex-*Essence* cover girl Simone Casey. I met her through our book as she was writing for *Who* magazine. We stayed in touch via Facebook and when I announced I was pregnant she immediately encouraged me to join. Initially I thought she was jumping the gun and wondered why on earth I'd need a support group or any education. I'm glad Simone persisted and one of my subsequent 1800mum2mum calls saved my life. Hormones flying everywhere and in such confusion about controlled crying from a book I now think should be illegal, I picked up the phone to an angel—Janet Murphy, who ended up being a huge source of support. She told me to let the tears flow as it helped the milk to flow and that my son needed to see my real feelings as I was afraid of crying in front of him. Janet stayed on the phone to me and I told her about my fear of letting him fall asleep on the breast. He was happy there though. I looked down and baby Beaudy had fallen asleep. I asked Janet as I held him in one arm and phone in the other, "What should I do now?" She said, "Do you have to go to work today?" I replied, "No" and she asked, "How old is he?" I said "Nine weeks." She said "Just hold him. He's not going to be nine weeks ever again!" That afternoon I held him with a warm feeling in my heart that erased the other fear that he would always need to be held to be able to fall asleep. Our breathing synchronised and I was in as much bliss as he. I have tears of gratitude for the ABA team as I write. Each time I have a tough day, I tell myself to hold him as he won't be a baby ever again. It was my new mantra. It still is. Day by day, moment by moment with the gentle parenting that Pinky McKay taught me to flow with and I see now how important it is for the government to put the new parental leave legislation in place so mums have time to bond.

So you see, breastfeeding and the ABA is so much more than feeding. My natural birth and this experience has given me the start to a life of attached parenting with a family bond for life. It takes a village to raise a child? The ABA is my village.

Creative Village Tips

Of course, you may not want to give up your job completely or at all. We may not want our mothers, mother-in-laws, sisters and aunties all moving in to create 'the village' either, but surely there's a middle ground for all of us somewhere.

You can create your own village by gathering around you the people who want to help to do the things that give you more time with your baby. This way you can get to know its needs, see when it needs help to go to the toilet, or learn its tired and hungry cues. The only way you can connect and learn these things is by spending time with them. So having your loved ones do your domestic duties like cooking, cleaning, helping you to shower, eat or sleep for an hour or so in the day will really help you. Most of the time people want to help but land up just wanting to hold the baby for you while you do those jobs. They naturally want the 'fun' job! However, in the long run it doesn't really help because you don't get to recover. You also feel like you've missed out on holding your baby in the early days.

The above are mainly primal needs much like the needs of the new addition. There's no 'one size fits all' magic solution to more sleep and when your baby should feed. Only you will know that and you will get really good at it in time too.

Five Easy Things to Help You Cope

1. Carry your baby

By wearing your baby in a sling or carrier, you can create a special bond by being close, get to know their needs more, allow them to feel safe and secure, create movement for the developing brain or for them to fall asleep to. There are so many different ways you can wear your baby. There are wraps, which is the way the Africans wear them; your baby can be in a variety of positions this way. A sling is nice and easy and great for the first 3-5 months, maybe more depending on the size of your baby. This keeps them in the foetal position, which is better, for at least the first 3 months. Carriers that require your baby to have legs open and fit you like a back pack on your front or back are probably best for after 3-4 months. In terms of the development of the pelvis, being in this position for too long isn't ideal. When they are a little older, look for carriers that will be better for your back and hold up to 20kg. A recommended one is the ERGO Baby Carrier, but it's just a matter of looking at all the different ones and seeing which is right for you.

2. Get to know your neighbours and community

You have a 'village' of people in your neighbourhood. If you don't have family to help in the first year or so, you'll be amazed how many people would really love to help you that may be right next door, literally. It may mean they take your dog and baby for a walk while you get an hour of shut eye, or come to visit you for a cup of tea and rock your baby to sleep for you while you do some domestic duties!. Better still, you may have a neighbour offer to do some ironing or cut your grass. One of the nicest presents we got was when a friend of ours mowed the lawn for us when our son was first born. It was such a great feeling driving into the driveway and noticing his gift. It is these small acts of kindness that really help and allow you to spend more time with your baby, which is what your baby needs. A nice person will recognise that. Start to get to know who you have around you and work at creating a little community. I'm sure you'd do the same for them in a time of need too. There'll be plenty of time to return the favour. There are also many groups you can join that have the same values as you in parenting. These groups can provide emotional support in trying times as well as other creative ideas about how to help each other.

3. Ask for help

Don't be embarrassed at all to ask for help. If a neighbour offers assistance then open your heart, swallow your pride and accept it. You are not meant to pretend you have it all under control and don't need help remember? If there was ever a time to delegate; now is it. Is there someone you could be asking who can do something for you? It may be a colleague you haven't spoken to since birth, a family friend or someone in your extended social circle.

There's a movement called Attached Parenting (AP) that allows parents to discuss and feel supported in ways that give them the confidence to parent in an attached manner. You may like to see if the online forums suit you and your family. At the very least, you could get some great ideas from these people that you can use, or get some questions answered. The only way to find out is to ask.

4. Create a meal group

Cooking healthy meals can be really time consuming. It takes time to wash and prepare vegetables. You may not even have the energy to make something let alone be inspired to make something new. Let's face it, meals can often taste better just because someone else has cooked it. A great idea a friend told me once is to get a group of friends or neighbours together and have a day of the week that you cook for each other. On a weekly visit, one friend will drop off a meal that they have made for themselves as well as you and your whole family. That way, when it's your turn to cook; you just cook a little bit extra for them and look forward to your night off from cooking the next night.

5. Use your time off work wisely

A strict routine isn't natural, so you need to stay at home most of the time, at least in the beginning. But for many women being at home alone is difficult. Where's the village? And why am I eating a 'guilt sandwich'?

It's important to allow yourself to enjoy the time off you have from work and other obligations. If you are the kind of woman that does too much then now really is the time to cut yourself some slack.

> **Five Easy things to Help you Cope**
> - 1. Carry your baby
> - 2. Get to know your neighbours and community
> - 3. Ask for help
> - 4. Create a meal group
> - 5. Use your time off work wisely

Chapter Seven

Baby Sleep Tips & Myths

"People who say they sleep like a baby usually don't have one."
— Leo J. Burke

Okay, so now we understand that babies wake often at night and it's natural. We also have the knowledge and certainty that we need to be responsive parents, attending to our babies no matter what time. But how do we manage in this Western world where we have jobs and domestic duty responsibilities? Night-time parenting presents mothers with a great surprise. If you know to expect that the baby will wake up a lot, you will feel more peaceful about it and find a way to get more sleep for yourself.

The amount of feeding at night varies with each baby, but most babies who are fully responded to will wake up often as it's natural and healthy. The baby grows rapidly when asleep and is therefore frequently hungry. Interestingly, most African and Aboriginal mothers don't even think of "putting" a baby to sleep and don't even 'put them down'. The mother just goes about her life with the baby on her body. The baby sleeps on and off, developing bodily self-awareness and self-reliance. At night the mother will lay down with the baby expecting to wake up as needed.

Such constant physical connection seems daunting to modern mothers. The difficulty arises when we resist the way the baby is. We then focus on fixing her ways, instead of responding to the way she is. Try not to change your baby; see what he is rather than trying to make him something he is not. We can explore a middle ground again where we can find ways to help you get some sleep and incorporate some natural ways of working with your baby that may help them sleep better.

Natural Sleep Solutions

Magic Chiropractic

What is Chiropractic? Chiropractic is safe, gentle and unbelievably effective. It is also the third largest health-care system in the world. It is the art of healing that unleashes the innate ability of the body to heal itself by realigning the spine. This opens the nerve channels and allows the healing power of your body to be turned on. The nervous system is the 'master controller' of your body. Through a nervous system free of interference, the brain sends and receives all the vital and correct messages your body needs to function with. Chiropractic is drugless. In fact, it is the fastest growing healing profession in the world that doesn't use drugs or surgery.

Babies, adults and the elderly may all experience complete life enhancement through chiropractic. Through chiropractic your children could grow up with as much assistance as possible to meet the forthcoming challenges. It is never too soon to experience the benefits.

The removal of nerve interference by chiropractic adjustment restores the normal curves of the spine.

Shifts in your spine are commonly called subluxations. Subluxations are the silent destroyers of your health. How you feel is a poor judge of your health. By the time a symptom appears, many spinal problems are advanced. Chiropractic focuses on the damaging importance of subluxation — a loss of normal spinal and nervous system function — essential to all body systems such as the immune system.

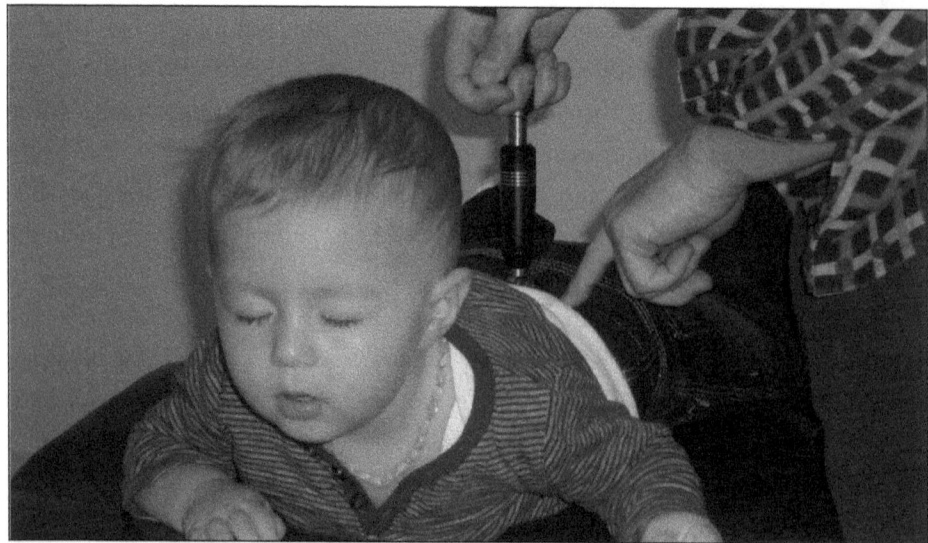

Beaudy getting an adjustment from his dad

The art of chiropractic is thousands of years old. In 1895, in the US, Dr DD Palmer was searching for the cause of disease and explored many types of healing arts. One day his janitor, who had been partially deaf for many years, allowed Palmer to examine him. No one previously discovered what Palmer did — a lump in his neck from a shifted spinal bone (subluxation). Palmer convinced the janitor to allow him to 'adjust' the shifted bone to its normal position using his hands. The janitor's hearing was restored and chiropractic as we know it today was born.

So how can it help your child?

Paediatric chiropractic is fast becoming a must- do for all those parents wanting to give their baby the best start in life. Even with a natural birth, our first vertebral subluxation (Spinal misalignment and nerve system interference) can begin here. Modern birthing techniques often involve pulling and twisting on the head and neck. There's also the consideration of your baby's position inside the womb. Often the baby may engage early or get stuck in a position towards the end of the pregnancy and you can imagine what can happen if intervention is needed.

Many authorities suggest that the position of the mother coupled with the pulling from the delivering physician has a lot to do with the creation of these subluxation-related problems. When the delivering mother is lying on her back she is not only working partially against gravity but she has reduced the pelvic opening size. These two factors then require the attending physician to pull harder on the head of the child. This increased pulling and twisting during the birth process, coupled with a decrease in the pelvic opening and a non-alignment with gravity, often set the stage for birth trauma, subluxation and resulting problems. It is exceptionally common that changes during pregnancies, including the mother having pre-existing pelvic problems, may bring about vertebral subluxation in babies.

Vertebral subluxation is a condition where the bones of the spine malfunction or misalign and choke, stretch or irritate the delicate spinal nerves.

This nerve interference has been implicated in many health problems. A study published in the German medical journal *Manual Medicine* involved a group of 1,258 babies who had their spines examined by two medical doctors within five days of birth. Of this group, 211 suffered from vomiting, hyperactivity or sleeplessness. Manual examination of the babies revealed spinal abnormalities in 95% of the group. The authors recommend spinal adjustments and note that they "... frequently resulted in immediate quieting, cessation of crying, muscular relaxation and sleepiness".[1]

The authors noted that vertebral subluxation in the upper neck area caused "many

---

[1] Gutman G. Blocked Atlantal Nerve Syndrome in Babies and Infants. Manuelle Medizin. 1987;25:5-10

clinical features from central motor impairment and development (sleeplessness, incoordination, seizures) through ... impairments of vegetative regulatory systems (vomiting, digestive problems, elimination problems), to lowered resistance to infections, especially to ear, nose and throat infection.

As a result of this research, many experts are now suggesting that birth be handled as a normal and natural process. One of their suggestions is for the birthing position of choice to be an upright position of sitting or squatting, using gravity to assist the birth process. This would result in less force being used for delivery and reduce the trauma from birth and the subluxation-related effects.

With the suction, forceps and drugs that can impact on mum and baby at birth, chiropractic can be a god-send, literally."

> **Here are some common signs and symptoms that can indicate your baby might be having some spinal and/or cranial issues which chiropractic can help with:**
> - Breast feeding issues
> - Poor suck or attachment
> - Excessive crying or fussing.
> - Easily startled
> - Preferring one breast over another
> - Difficulty sleeping
> - Sleeping in the same head position all the time
> - Excessive dislike to tummy time
> - Misshapen head or a flat part on the head
> - Asymmetrical facial features
> - Medical intervention used during birth.

Unlike the techniques used on an adult for removing vertebral subluxation and nerve system interference, chiropractic adjustments for babies gently realign the spine, pelvis and cranial bones. The pressure it may take to adjust your baby and correct alignment may be as gentle as if you had to place your finger on your eye ball, just like when putting on a contact lens. It's not the amount for pressure or force, but the specific and scientific location and correction and intention of the chiropractic adjustment and alignment. This re-alignment allows for optimum nerve flow and development which in turn allows optimal function of every cell, tissue and organ in your baby's body. The nervous system is responsible for how you perceive the world, adapt to stress and co-ordinate all body parts. The nervous system controls every organ, cell and tissue in the body, including the immune system, muscular system and other nine systems. This is why chiropractic care may help with such a wide range of health challenges your baby may have.

You also may benefit from having chiropractic care, which can help you settle your baby better. A difficult pregnancy, birth or breastfeeding issues, carrying other children and stress or sleepless nights can all impact on your nervous system, not to mention possible pre-existing vertebral subluxation you may have. Making sure your spine is free of misalignment may help you to relax, and be able rock your baby without discomfort or create a better environment for a let-down to occur while breastfeeding. It also may help you to sleep better. By having a chiropractic adjustment, you can switch off the overactive nervous system which may allow you to have better quality sleep.[2]

Baby Accessory

The new necklace is your baby! You may not be able to wear the same fashion you used to as a little person will be pulling at your earrings; so the best accessory you will wear will be the little human you made!

Wearing your baby is a way to meet many needs. 'Baby-wearing' is an instinctive parenting style where your baby is held close to you in a sling, wrap or pouch for most of the day. It gives a busy parent the freedom to continue their normal daily routine while providing the most nourishing and desirable environment for a child.

Social conditioning has led parents to believe that if a baby is held or carried too frequently they will be spoilt, clingy or demanding. Modern research reveals quite the opposite. The physical and psychological benefits associated with baby wearing encourage children to feel secure and content and build a solid sense of self-esteem.

Baby-wearing calms fussy babies and helps decrease the occurrence of postnatal depression. The closeness enables parents to respond to baby's signals, which results in less frustration and stress, more confidence as a parent and most of all, less crying for all parties involved.

It not only promotes an intimate connection, but it promotes good digestion, which is believed to greatly ease the distressing symptoms of colic and reflux.

Babies worn in slings are less clingy and tend to initiate separation much earlier

---

[2] *How Chiropractic Works in your Sleep* study

than babies less frequently held. It allows them to be AT the centre of activity, not THE centre of attention, which is a wonderful environment proven to stimulate brain development and cognitive learning.

The benefits of wearing your baby:
- Security in attachment through mutual regulation of temperature, heart beat and breathing
- Necessary movement your baby requires to develop the vestibular and nervous system
- Keeping baby close means your milk supply can stay strong
- Keeping baby close means you can respond to signals before they start crying. This allows for a happier baby and a more relaxed and empowered parent.

Other benefits for you mean you get to:
- Bond with your baby, which develops trust in your relationship
- Strength and fitness benefits because of the extra weight
- Promoted weight loss as a result of increasing the physical load
- You can get a lot of work or chores done as you have free hands when you wear your little one
- Allow baby to fall asleep on you anytime, anywhere

Similarly, do not put your baby into a seat that helps them to sit. These are the plastic or rubber chairs often called 'Bumbo' seats. You are encouraging your baby to sit in an upright position before they are actually ready.

Rocking and Bouncing

Despite what other authors and 'baby trainers' may tell you about not relying on a sleeping aid to settle your baby– there's nothing wrong with it. Not only do you need a sleeping aid to get to sleep most nights, but babies need it for brain development reasons that are so beneficial. Think about the hot shower you have or the warm drink you consumed before bed. Did you read a good book or talk to your partner about the

CHAPTER SEVEN - BABY SLEEP TIPS & MYTHS

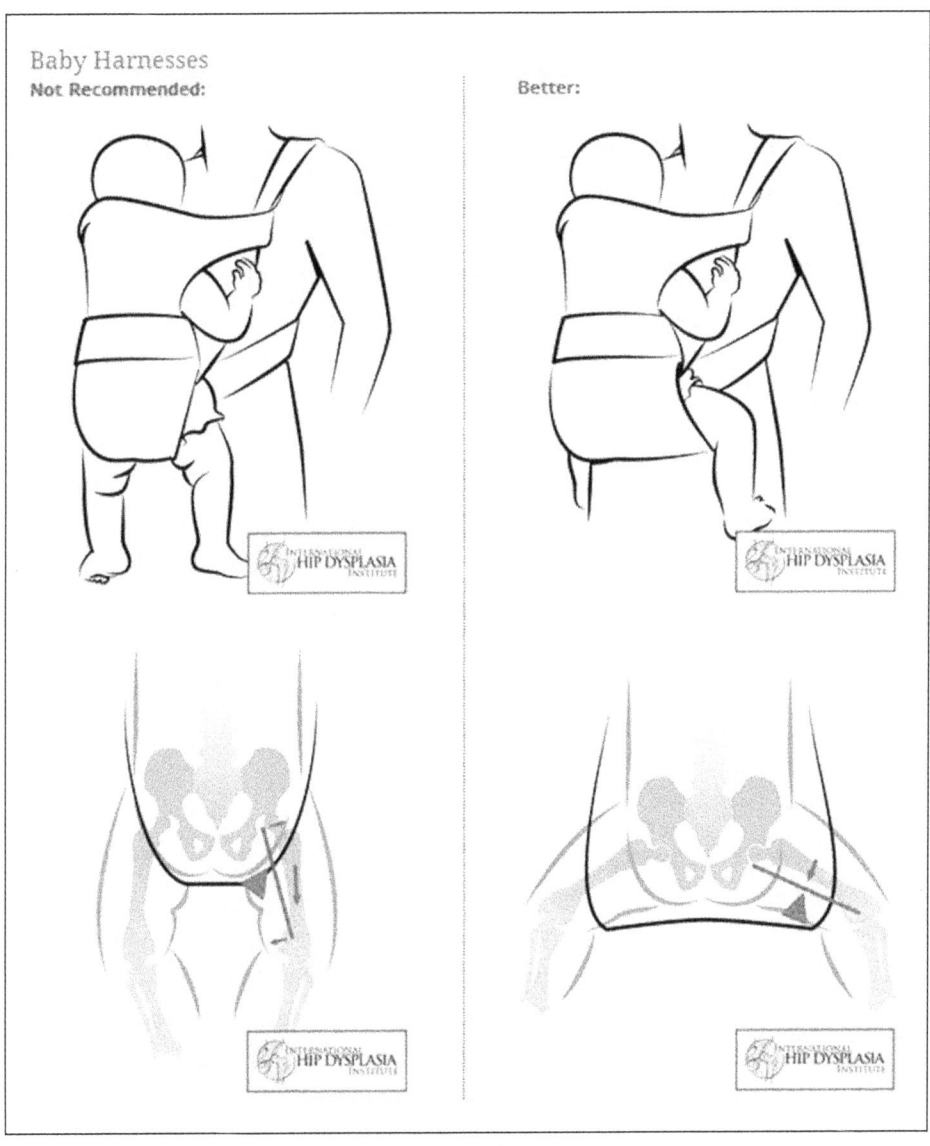

Baby Harnesses
Not Recommended: Better:

day's events? Perhaps you listened to some music or had a cuddle? All of these things help you to fall asleep in a more relaxed way and your baby is exactly the same.

Your baby though has and needs something I wish I could still have — rocking to sleep! Have you ever wished someone could sweep you off your feet after a tough day and rock you to sleep? On holidays do you rush to the hammock in the sunshine and doze off listening to the sounds of the ocean? There are reasons we love rocking and babies especially love it, because it's not just nice, but imperative for the development of the vestibula part of the brain. The vestibula needs rocking for optimal development. When someone has handed a baby over to you, notice how you naturally start swaying? We too are wired to respond this way. I once saw a woman with a baby on her hip at the supermarket. She had a shopping trolley in the other hand and was rocking the shopping trolley back and forth. It was filled with nothing but groceries, which must have been having a grand time! She didn't even realise she was looking very funny. So, what comes naturally to you is what you are meant to do. You can start by rocking a baby in your arms. You may like to use a rocking chair, or we found that a fit ball or 'Swisse' ball worked wonders, because we could sit on it when we got tired or he felt heavy and we could 'bounce' Beaudy to sleep. It was quite meditative for all parties involved. Basically any movement is good, so whether it's a ball, your arms or the car or pram, create the scenario because they love it and it's good for them.

Only transfer them if you have to. After a pram walk to sleep, I would leave baby in there to sleep and take a nap on the couch near the door. You may like to leave your monitor near the pram and nap on your bed. If they're in the car, you may have a seat that you can remove and bring in with you. But I've been known to park the car, put the driver's seat all the way back and take a nap in the car too; falling asleep to the sound of my baby's gentle and beautiful, tiny breathing pattern!

Handy Hammock

Hammocks are a wonderful way of incorporating movement and sleep into your baby's world. Because your baby was used to being inside you with constant movement for its first nine months, he finds it very settling to fall asleep with movement. There are so many types of hammocks around now that you will be sure to find one that is right for you. Despite what others say, a hammock is very safe. You can go to the SIDS website for more information on safe hammock sleeping. When Beaudy got heavy and didn't fit in his hammock anymore, we decided to rock him to sleep and wait until he was completely asleep before we put him down onto a flat surface. He got very heavy so we would sit him in our laps and bounce on a fit ball. This made it much easier and he loved it. One day I searched high and low for a larger hammock and finally found a wonderful store full of natural parenting ideas. As I fantasised about being rocked to sleep myself that day. I asked the store owner if she new of any really big hammocks for babies? She said: "Why don't you just buy a real hammock? That's how they do it in Asian countries." It was like a light bulb moment. I remembered a friend of mine used to tie a big hammock from one end of the tree in her garden to her granny flat where she and her child lived. She is a super single mum. She would swing her son to sleep several times a day. I'm sure she got the idea from her international friends.

She said people in Asian countries have been known to put their babies in giant hammocks tied up to trees and sway them to sleep. American Indians have also been carrying their babies around in a papoose, which is just like a hammock and emulates the sensation of still being in the womb. To think they were all doing it for centuries and we have been missing out all this time.

Womb Sounds – White Noise

Other ways of emulating the womb so that your baby feels secure is by playing some white noise which sends its brain into an Alpha state. Do you recall sitting on a plane and for some reason every time there's take off, half the people on the plane are asleep by the time it's in the air? It's because of the constant drone. The noise on the plane is perfect 'white noise' for sleeping. There are many CDs available that aim to provide white noise for your baby or the same beat as a heart beat with two four and four, four timing. However, you can tap into your intuition for other ideas. One day I came back from a walk with Beaudy asleep in the pram. To keep him asleep I parked the pram near the range hood above the oven. Others have turned on their vacuum for a while or clothes dryer. I am always grateful for next door neighbours mowing their lawns as it provides wonderful white noise for us to sleep to.

Meditate

I found that with each breastfeed, it became more and more apparent that I was meditating him to sleep. It felt like a time and space to be and not think or do, but totally be in the moment and at one with each other. I later learned there are hormones that are released while feeding that make you not have a care in the world besides that of your baby's wellbeing. You can create this even if you are not breastfeeding by focussing only on them and you and the act of nourishing your baby not just with 'food', but with love. One woman explained to me that breastfeeding to her was like she melted her heart and poured it into his mouth. Liquid love? Mmmm … sounds good, huh? It's all about intention and your loving intent is so powerful. Just by being with your baby and being in the moment with them is a meditation.

Synchronise Heart and Breath

You actually don't really need to try too hard to do this. You'll find that as you feed your baby, you're synchronising heart beat and breathing. This is like a form of meditation but it's actually mutual regulation and so healthy for the baby. I discovered it had great health benefits for the feeder too. How could you not benefit from beautiful breathing and relaxation several times a day. It kind of forces you to relax and we all know that we Western women do too much anyway. You'll find that if you have somewhere to be or are having to leave the baby with the babysitter or even if your mind is on a job you need to do, instead of being in the moment, your baby may start to fuss and it may be harder to settle them. It's because not only is your mind elsewhere but because it is, your heart beat may race or at the very least not be in synch with your baby and they will feel it. Try to stay in the moment and remember how much your baby loves you and how soft his skin feels and get back to just 'being'.

Happy Mum, Happy Baby

It's really important to look after you and setting up a community or network of people around you is paramount to the health and wellbeing of the mother. Mums find it hard enough making choices like having to go back to work and suffer with enough guilt about the way they parent. If a mother chooses to parent 'naturally' in a very responsive and 'attached' manner that is gentle to the baby's cues and follows the baby's lead, then she and her partner must get creative and find ways in which her community and family can support that. The reality is that we don't live in a 'village'. We live far away from each other, separately in big houses. Parenting naturally requires a village of people. You can create your own village. This will help you have some time to look after you.

I had a friend who separated from the father of her child very early on, in fact while she was pregnant. She found it very difficult and challenging at times raising her child on her own in many ways, including financially. This, one would imagine, is a huge problem. But this friend found a way to make the problem the solution. She managed to find a share house arrangement where she could rent the granny flat and the others that lived in the house became her 'village' and helped become a family to her child. It's a perfect example of where the problem, became the solution in trying times as she had access to others who could help her take care of herself too.

There are other ways to gain emotional support and with the World Wide Web, we can access many websites and blogs where parents can swap ideas, give advice and share what works for them. Many mothers are flocking to this way of communicating because it can be done at any time of the day, in a track suit and perhaps even typing with one finger while breastfeeding with the other arm.

Here's a beautiful candid blog from a mother who shared her heart with me and others on Facebook one bleary eyed night.

Karen- mother of one:

> *I think this is the time where gentle parenting mothers have a hard time sharing how tough it can get. I know I have days where I begin to feel exactly like 'they' said I would (rod in back etc). My son is a total breast addict - feeding to sleep day and night and needing the breast to resettle, day and night. I stay at home so it really isn't a problem, but the endless demands on me and my body does get draining. There are very few people who understand that even though we chose to mother this way (because we followed our hearts), it doesn't mean we don't need to share the journey and find support through the trying times. I'm finding that as my son nears 2, I'm questioning myself as I did when he was a newborn... like, 'shouldn't he be sleeping without me by now?" When in fact: I love our co-sleeping arrangement. We seek each other out to help us find our own ways of dealing with the transitions of baby to toddler because we don't follow what some random 'expert' tells us. Thanks, rant over!"*

Magical Magnesium

Apart from taking care of you emotionally, there are some things you can do nutritionally that will help you with your adrenal system, which at times will be running overtime.

It's important to make sure your diet is filled with as many fresh and live foods so that you too will be nourished with life.

Vitamin B and magnesium have been particularly important for new mothers to replenish their stores and help to relax. A good B complex helps to revitalise energy stores and reinvigorate a depleted nervous system. Essential fatty acids are another supplement imperative for new mums and we cover them in more detail in the pages to come.

A good naturopath will be able to assess your whole health and address what it is you need but as a rule here are the benefits of the most forgotten and overlooked super supplements.

We all know the benefits of vitamin C and have been educated enough to know we must stock up on the supplement to boost our immune system especially during the winter months. Advertising has done its job in educating us about the importance of calcium to prevent osteoporosis. But did you know that magnesium is vital for normal muscle and nervous system function? That's pretty important for a new mother to consume if she's going to want to function at her best.

To make it even more important to ingest, did you know that all your organs are muscles too? If your body is lacking in magnesium, it affects the way your entire body functions. Together with calcium they act to bring about muscle contraction and relaxation. A balance of both is imperative for a healthy body. Most people meet their calcium requirements and it's very important to get those from plenty of dark greens. The big mistake is that we often fail to consume optimal amounts of magnesium. It's not just for athletes. Some mothers-to-be complain of restless leg syndrome and muscle cramping in their legs during pregnancy, especially at night. To avoid muscle cramps, take extra magnesium. It will certainly help and feed all your muscles with the nutrition it requires to function at its best during pregnancy and of course in the first few challenging year. I hear many breastfeeding mothers talk of how it helped their babies feel relaxed too as they were able to access it from the milk.

Like all super heroes that always have a big job ahead of them, magnesium too, has its work cut out for it! Another important role this 'super supplement' plays is to help with calcium absorption. Good quality powder form is best and can be obtained from your naturopath or chiropractor. Working with these professionals that deal with your muscular, nervous system and digestive system all day every day, means that you get a holistic look at healing and feeding your body with the right nutrition.

In the last couple of years, there has been a number of sports drinks that have been marketing the benefits of magnesium. It's easy to understand the benefits of the more common electrolytes found in these drinks, but what is this new magnesium craze all about?

My Melbourne chiropractor husband, Dr. Warren Sipser says:

> "As a keen cyclist and performance enhancing chiropractor, I am always searching for improved ways to better my own scores as well as those of the athletes who seek my care. Chiropractic offers athletes and 'weekend warriors' the opportunity to function at their genetic maximum by removing any interferences affecting their nerve systems. It is the only profession that focuses on the delicate relationship between the performance of the nerve system and how the spine can interfere with normal function. While not all magnesium is created equal, a highly soluble, good quality form can aid enormously in not only your power and stamina, but also your recovery time."

We are running our own little marathon every day and night as a new parent, healing from birth and learning about our new role. If magnesium is the agonist and antagonist to the much publicised calcium and both are needed for active muscle contractions and relaxations, then let's take a look at what the current studies have to say:

- A study of male athletes supplemented with 390mg of magnesium per day for 25 days resulted in an increased peak oxygen uptake and total work output during work capacity tests.
- A sub-maximal work study, showed that magnesium supplementation reduced heart rate, ventilation rate, oxygen uptake and carbon dioxide production for a given workload.
- A study on physically active students, which showed that supplementing with 8mg of magnesium per kilo of body weight per day produced significant increases in endurance performance and decreased oxygen consumption during sub-maximal exercise.
- A magnesium shortfall also appears to reduce the efficiency of muscle relaxation, which accounts for an important fraction of total energy needs during exercise.
- Magnesium supplementation could enhance performance in a hitherto unrecognised way – by reducing the accumulation of fatiguing lactic acid during intense exercise.
- The researchers concluded that "magnesium supplement may positively affect performance of sportsmen by decreasing their lactate levels".
- Magnesium lends credence to its importance in overall physical, mental and emotional well-being.

The Science and Why it Matters

Pure magnesium is the second most abundant mineral in cells after potassium, but the 2oz or so found in the typical human body is present not as metal but as magnesium ions (positively charged magnesium atoms found either in solution or complexed with other tissues such as bone). Roughly one-quarter of this magnesium is found in muscle tissue and three-fifths in bone, but less than 1% of it is found in blood serum, although blood magnesium is used as the commonest indicator of magnesium status. This blood serum magnesium can further be subdivided into free ionic, complex-bound and protein-bound portions, but it's the ionic portion that's considered most important in measuring magnesium status, because it is physiologically active.

The researchers concluded that not only did supplemental magnesium help suppress lactate production, but that it also somehow increased glucose availability and metabolism in the brain during exercise. This is important because scientists now believe that the brain and central nervous system play a large role in determining the degree of muscular fatigue we feel, higher brain glucose availability could in theory translate into lower levels of perceived fatigue.

So before you think you need chocolate or sugar (which is more addictive than heroin), to keep you going, try a spoonful of magnesium in water to balance your body instead.

Antioxidant and anti-inflammatory activity

Another study looked at lung function and in particular whether dietary antioxidants might protect lung tissue against reactive oxygen species-induced injury, adverse respiratory effects and reduced pulmonary function. Healthy, non-smoking freshmen students who were lifetime residents in the Los Angeles or the San Francisco Bay areas of California completed comprehensive residential history, health history and food frequency questionnaires. Blood samples were also collected and forced expiratory volume (lung power) measurements were obtained. Using a statistical technique called multivariable regression, the researchers showed that the higher the intake of dietary magnesium, the more positive the lung function (indicating healthier more elastic lung tissue).

A third study published just a few months ago examined the effect of magnesium supplementation on inflammatory markers in patients with chronic heart disease. The study, conducted by Israeli researchers, compared the levels of the inflammatory marker C-reactive protein in patients given 300mg a day of magnesium citrate with a control group given no magnesium.

The result showed unequivocally that the extra magnesium produced a significant drop in C-reactive protein levels, indicating reduced inflammation, so much so that the researchers commented that "targeting the inflammatory cascade by magnesium administration might prove a useful tool for improving the prognosis in heart failure".

Some foods high in this wonderful mineral are -

- Seeds and nuts such as almonds
- Unrefined whole grains, such as wholemeal bread and whole grain cereals
- Peas, beans and lentils
- Dark green leafy vegetables such as kale, spinach and silverbeet.

Contrary to popular belief, milk and dairy products are not particularly rich sources of magnesium. Magnesium is a fairly soluble mineral, which is why boiling vegetables can result in significant losses, in cereals and grains. It tends to be concentrated in the germ and bran, which explains why white refined grains contain relatively little magnesium by comparison with their unrefined counterparts.

A diet rich in colour and with minimal packaged foods are best. The healthiest thing you can eat is putting something in your mouth that is close to nature as possible.

Try growing some kale for this winter season and stock up on your new super supplements.

Keep Close

At around 3-4 months old, your baby is starting to have a developmental growth spurt. These growth spurts can happen at any age and continue to happen as your baby takes the world in around them. It's at this time that they are becoming aware of what is happening. For example, they are now understanding that it is a glass of water that mama is holding to her lips and can see much more that it is sometimes, as you can imagine, very scary and overwhelming. You will notice that you may need to tell your baby as it gets a little older that you are leaving the room and will be coming back. Your baby doesn't know yet about this and thinks you are leaving them for good. Distance and space are being learned among other things and unfamiliar or strange and toxic smells like perfume or cigarettes and alcohol can be unsettling. Not only are they foreign and not you, but they are chemicals that can upset a baby. Your baby pretty much thinks it's still attached to you for around nine months after it comes out of you. That's why some say that separation anxiety can be at its greatest at this time as they realise they are separate. Therefore, up until nine months old, keeping baby close to you by holding them or wearing them or sleeping next to them is great for mother and baby in so many ways. For breastfeeding mothers especially, the more you hold and feed your baby in the day, the greater the chances of them waking to be held at night.

Family Bath

Having a bath together is another way of keeping close and the skin-to-skin contact is excellent for immune building too. The water and warmth emulates what it was like to be in your womb and the experience is oh so comforting. It also relaxes you, the parents, which contributes to a better sleep for you. It's great to make time for a bath, no matter what the reason, so enjoy your daily or nightly ritual together at least once a week. You can usually keep them asleep if they are falling asleep during a feed. If you find that trying to bring up wind with them is waking them too much, don't worry about it as they may need to go to sleep and either pass it through the other end later or wake up, but when you pick them up for a cuddle, they pass wind at the same time, resolving the issue and allowing them to sleep. The benefit of not letting your baby cry before a feed is that they are more relaxed, their tongue isn't in spasm and they can latch and attach properly and may take in less air when feeding. Not to mention the trust it creates as you, through your actions, teach your baby that he doesn't need to act dramatically to get your attention. You show him you understand his unique language and that his needs and feelings are valid.

Remove Blue Light and EMFs

A natural way of falling to sleep, baby or adult, is to allow the lunar (moon) cycle to guide us. Our bodies naturally want to fall asleep with the dark and wake with the light. It's what the universe or 'god' has created to help us relax and wake.

Shining or putting a light and in particular a blue light near your baby, can arouse them or wake them from a sleep cycle. This includes things like lights from alarm clocks and mobile phones. We may also use a lap top, computer or i-pad or i-phone that emits these kinds of lights, not to mentions electromagnetic fields (EMFs).

You see, to be able to fall asleep naturally, the human body produces melatonin, a hormone created in the pineal gland. This hormone allows your body to relax enough to sleep. It also follows the lunar cycle and natural circadian rhythm. These blue lights and interferences make it very hard for the body to get into that relaxed state and fall asleep naturally.

You may be wondering why, in particular, the colour blue? It's a colour highly visible in the daytime, giving you a cue to wake up, which is pretty bad if it's sleep you want. Those technological gadgets emit the blue light that reduces melatonin production.

Avoid using your computer or watching television before bed. Try not to use your mobile phone as a torch to see your baby. By avoiding blue light in the evening and right before bed, you can help your body produce the optimal amount of melatonin and you can fall asleep in a natural way. You will find this to be a much healthier sleep too.[3]

---

3 http://www.marksdailyapple.com/17-w...
   https://www.lowbluelights.com/index.asp?
   http://stereopsis.com/flux/
   http://news.bioscholar.com/2007/11/...

Cuddle Confidence is Key

By being a responsive parent, picking up your baby or at least attending to them, you allow yourself a greater chance to be able to discover what it is that your baby needs. Babies usually want to be picked up and be held by you to feel safe to do things like burp, vomit or just pass wind or have a bowel motion. Another reason your baby may want to be picked up is to get in a vertical position to take the pressure off their gums while teething. Being in a horizontal position puts more pressure on the gums and picking your baby up to rock them back to sleep is a natural way of helping through the teething phase. Being vertical is pretty necessary to be able to get a burp up too so if your baby wakes after he has just fallen asleep, you may find it is to burp. The only way to know what it is your baby needs, is to actually pick them up and give them a cuddle and the rest will follow.

You will find that the more you cuddle and the more you discover what your baby's needs are by cuddling them and picking them up out of their bed, you will gain more confidence as a parent and they too will gain more confidence and self-esteem, not to mention trust in their relationship with you. Finally, if your baby is waking or crying out to be picked up, and it isn't to fart, burp or for teething, then at the very least you get a cuddle; your baby must just want to cuddle you. It's a great problem to have. Just enjoy! This phase too shall pass and try to think about ho much you are helping them to develop neurologically and emotionally by responding gently.

Comforting Smells

If your baby is going to be in another bed or room, make the transition gently to slowly get him used to being away from you. Help him to feel comfortable. There are many essential oil sprays that are marketed as 'relaxing room spray' and the like. You may want to make up your own with the essential oil lavender which has been known to have very calming and relaxing properties when inhaled in a diluted form. You could even put a few drops on a pillow or mattress. But the most comforting smell of all is you. Some mothers I know, and even a very cute father or two, have taken off the t-shirt or blouse that have worn that day and left it in the cot (safely, so that the baby won't end up moving it over their face. Tie it to the rails or stretch it over the mattress) to help the baby feel and smell you. It makes them feel like you are still close by. Even if the smell of your armpit seems rancid to you, it's actually heaven for your baby. They are comforted to know that you are close and then when they wake and call for you and you come, the trust in your relationship continues to develop.

Some mothers leave their brassiere so that the smell of their milk is the comfort. You may like to try this. It has been known to work for some, but all babies are different and at the end of the day, there is no substitute for you.

Teething Aids

Teething can be one of the hardest times of your child's life which can make it the most wakeful time. It affects their digestive system and immune system too which is why you may notice looser bowel movements, constipation or even diarrhea. Giving a baby drugs / medication should always be a last resort, or for emergency care only. You and your baby can deal with this natural transition naturally if you choose. There are so many tools and things you can use to help make teething more comfortable.

Amber beads — a semi-precious stone used in teething necklaces or wrist bands — has been known for centuries to help teething. In Europe they are sold in pharmacies and are the 'norm'. To be worn from four months onward, the amber is said to rub off into the skin and provide an analgesic effect when teeth start to cut. Some parents claim they didn't even know teeth were coming, others report that it minimised the effects and symptoms, and the rest say they didn't know if it worked or not but were not willing to take the necklace off to see if it was worse. None the less; the necklaces are safe and look very cute.

Bella Donna and Chamomilla homeopathic pills or liquid

Raising them up and propping them up when sleeping with a pillow in the cot is another great way to help ease the pain. Just like when you have a cold and your sinuses are blocked up, it is uncomfortable to lie flat and easier to be propped up; apparently it is the same for a teether. It takes the pressure off that area when the head is slightly raised. This is why when your baby is teething, he may wake more frequently for a cuddle. It's because when you pick them up you put them in a vertical position that makes them more comfortable and they can fall back to sleep again.

Breast milk and feeding. It seems that breast is best for teethers. There's something oh so natural and soothing for your baby in a breastfeed. I always imagine there are analgesic properties in the milk like a magic juice that sends them into a deeper sleep. It's quick and easy and there are no tears for all parties involved.

Food Blues

The 'first food experience' for a baby is a very exciting time just like taking the first steps or saying the first words. It's important to understand how to introduce solids safely, slowly and gently.

Your baby's digestive system is developing at a maturity that allows for solid foods to be introduced in a scaled way. It's just like learning a language and learning or introducing it word by word. The slower you introduce food and solids, the kinder you are being to your baby's stomach and this has an overall impact on how they can regulate their bowels, moods and sleep.

Naturopath and former technical advisor of gastro-intestinal pathology, Nicholas Smith believes feeding your child healthily can avoid such conditions as eczema, asthma and auto-immune conditions.

He says: "I cannot stress enough the importance of allowing the digestive system to reach a certain stage of maturation before introducing solids in order to lay the foundations for good health for life."

Six months old is the perfect age to start introducing food and no sooner. Giving solid food sooner can interrupt the flora and fauna of the gut and may take exclusive breastfeeding of up to two weeks to restore the health of the gut.

Your baby's intestinal tract is paper thin and everything that goes in their mouth to the other end can have either a great impact or a bad one. Every food really does matter and so have a think very carefully about what you feed. It may help you to think very carefully about you feed yourself too. Your baby has already been getting a taste of foods through you from pregnancy. If you ate a wide variety of healthy foods during gestation, your baby will be familiar and open to try those foods too. This transcends into of course getting a taste for food through breast milk. Breast fed babies may be more open to trying different foods and especially all types of vegetables if you have been eating them as they have already tasted it through you.

Babies can get a big gulp of good bacteria that prepares their gut for good health as they pass through the vaginal canal. This is why ideally a vaginal birth is best because it sets up a foundation of good bacteria in the intestines which in turn primes the immune system. But don't worry if you had a c-section because your baby can get it all through breast milk. If you bottle feed and haven't had a vaginal birth, your baby can still develop good bacteria; it will just take longer and all the more reason to be careful with first foods. It's through the gut that immunity develops allowing your baby to have a less likely chance of developing hayfever, asthma, colds, constipation or diarrhea, which may also result in restless sleep.

Knowing not only when to start but what and how much is key too. Think about the animal kingdom again. A bird may squeeze tiny drops of food into the beak of her young. She doesn't start off with the whole food. If we were in a village in the days of the hunter and gatherer, we may only receive a few drops of a fruit from our mother as she devours the rest. She would share it slowly. The same fruit would probably be eaten for a whole week as they may have only picked one or two types. They consume only what is in season and what grows, moving onto another type of food when that becomes 'in season'. This is actually allowing the baby's gut to develop enzymes slowly to digest the new food. Moving on to new foods too fast doesn't allow a baby to get used to one food at a time or develop enzymes to digest it.

Start with six key foods for the first two months until the age of eight months-old.

It may seem like it is getting boring for you, but it isn't for your baby. The main thing is to also eat those foods yourself too.

The Australian Breastfeeding Association suggests BLS, which stands for baby-led solid feeding.

Gil Rapley is a midwife and breastfeeding counsellor and says:

> It's now over 7 years since the World Health Organization (WHO) published its recommendation that 6 months should be the earliest age for expanding a baby's diet beyond breast milk. The degree to which this recommendation has been embraced - by professionals as well as parents - varies hugely, with some choosing to ignore it altogether. But is it OK to start earlier if you're doing baby-led solids* (BLS)? This is a question that I am constantly asked and one which I find very hard to answer with a simple yes or no.
>
> The problem is that the words we use to talk about introducing solid foods just don't work when we're trying to explain BLS. What exactly do we mean by 'starting solids'? With the traditional (spoon-feeding) approach to introducing solids, the baby both meets and eats his first solid food in the same sitting - the two things happen only moments apart. So, not only is 'starting solids' easy to define but the parents know -- to the minute - exactly when it has happened.
>
> With BLS, there can be a time gap of several days or even weeks between the moment the baby first meets solid food and the moment when he first eats it. And the first food he meets may not be the first food he eats. And that's assuming we can even pinpoint exactly when the first 'meeting' took place. [4]

A baby-led approach consists of recognising the baby has been enticed by the smell of the food you consume. Perhaps he was in been in your arms feeding. He may have even tasted it through your milk. When he starts to hold himself up and sit up, this may suggest the readiness for solid food as it can indicate the readiness of the digestive

---

[4] Reproduced from 'Essence' magazine Volume 46 Number 1 Exclusively for ABA subscribers by Gill Rapley

system. It's also usually at this time that a baby has the motor skills to either turn his head away or push food away. This means they will show you when they have either had enough or are not ready for this type of food yet. Teeth can also suggest readiness for solid food. For example, your baby may not want meat or nuts until canines and molars are there. Drool is a pre-cursor to teething, which is a readiness for solids as the saliva is what digests the food. A diet of exclusively solid food will usually only take place once all teeth are through. Other than that, your baby relies on your breast milk as his main source of nutrition because you can make what he missed out on that day, meaning you don't have to worry about a wide varied diet as you are slowly introducing different foods.

Babies innately know what they need to eat. If they have consumed too many processed carbohydrates, you may notice them rejecting the next time you offer cereal and only wanting fruit. This is okay. You may find the next day after only wanting to consume pears, that your baby was constipated and needed this for excretion or immunity. A study was done in 1928 by paediatrician Clara Davis where a variety of different foods were laid out for the toddlers to try. As bizarre as this may sound, children were interested in eating only cod liver oil to boost their health. They chose this over thirty-four unrefined and wholesome foods.

Food Guide

Please note: *Every child is different and may show interest and readiness for certain foods a little earlier or later. This is a guide to help you find safe and non-reactive foods that prepare your child's digestive system slowly to get used to eating them and digesting them with ease.*

Introducing the wrong foods too early can cause reactions and allergies or upset stomachs. It's best to stick with the one new food that you introduced for at least 3 days before you introduce another to allow your baby to be able to develop enzymes to digest it. Then you will also notice if they are not responding well to it and may decide to avoid that particular food for a while. After exclusion, you can then re-introduce to see if they still react or if their gut is now ready.

During this precious time of introducing solids, please get a baby probiotic to mix with food to help the gut and digestion.

You may add water to juices to decrease sugar intake. Please add an essential fatty acid like a flax seed oil, cold pressed coconut, omega or cod liver oil to foods daily. These oils are essential for nerve system and brain development. They will help your baby's sleep too.

You may add breast milk or your formula to all foods. Please use an organic goat's formula right from birth if you are not breastfeeding. The human gut cannot digest the protein in cow's milk (casein): in adults the body creates a mucous coating to expel the casein through an orifice and in babies it may create anything from colic to reflux to skin rashes and sleeplessness or constipation. From 18 months onwards, you can switch to oat or rice milk.

Water is not needed initially if you are exclusively breastfeeding because your baby will be able to draw a watery type milk (foremilk) from your breasts to quench his thirst. You may like to offer solids before breastfeeding. It is very common for babies to then want a breastfeed to wash it down. One food is not a substitute for another during their first year.

If you are using formula, please offer water during and after meals.

6-8 months
- Avocado, stewed/steamed carrot, pumpkin sweet potato, banana, stewed pear. If you use rice, please use cooked brown rice, grounded.
- Amount: whatever lands in your baby's mouth or around 2 tablespoons and no more than this in total only 2-3 times a day
- Consistency: very smooth and blended

8-10 months
- Peaches, apples, nectarines, apricots, (if stone fruit is not in season, you don't need to offer this until it is) blackberries, blueberries, kiwi fruit, prunes, plums, cherries, oats, millet, quinoa cereal, egg yolk (the white is more difficult to digest and may be a reactive food) green beans, squash, broccoli.
- Amount: Around 4 tablespoons 3 times a day
- Consistency: a thicker puree

11-12 months
- Pineapple, papya, melons, peas, cauliflower, asparagus, buckwheat, amaranth, spelt, fish- (must be a small fish because larger fish have high levels of mercury in them as they eat smaller fish which also have mercury in them, hence higher quantities of mercury. Avoid shellfish for the first couple of years) yoghurt, fresh fruit and vegetable juices.
- Amount: Around 3-5 meals a day and self feeding or spoon feeding until baby loses interest or pushes the spoon away
- Consistency: a thicker mash

12-18 months
- Mango, strawberries, fresh figs, tomato, celery (frozen sticks are great for chewing on during teething) cucumber, spinach, artichoke, kamut, barley, wheat (although wheat may be avoided completely if you prefer a wheat free diet), rye, rice, noodles, meats, tahini, almond milk, maple syrup, organic honey (honey contains botulism), agave nectar, miso, organic nut butters- you can grind your own nuts in a processor to make pastes.
- Amount: Around several meals a day and self feeding or spoon feeding until baby loses interest or pushes the spoon away
- Consistency: a soft solid

18 months to 2 years
- Goats or sheeps cheese, all fruit, all vegetables, all grains, all dairy, whole eggs, all legumes and garlic.
- Your toddler will be able to feed himself and you should be offering something to eat every two-three hours or around six times a day. Once again be aware when they have had enough but always offer and let your baby guide you.
- Avoid refined cereals as a first food despite what all the supermarket packaging and advertising suggests.

Getting your baby involved in cooking right from birth is helpful to having them eventually like all types of healthy food. You may start by wearing your baby in a sling as you cook and then carry them on the hip as you stir, allowing them to see what you do; eventually your baby may like to stir and involving them in the process gets them excited as they develop a hunger around the smells. Your reaction to food is key too. If you sincerely love your vegetables, they will too. If you don't, you may like to try and find some new recipes. Going on a detox too can help your tastebuds develop a true taste for the sweetness of certain vegetables again too. Imagine you didn't consume one iota of sugar for two weeks? You would start to taste the sweetness of carrots again. This is what it is like for them. If you never give them sugar during the first couple of years, they will understand the true taste of foods. There are healthy alternatives like agave nectar and eventually honey and if you must introduce a little sugar in baking then raw sugar may be okay seldomly. But there's even stevia and xylitol which are plant-derived and better options for cooking. Avoiding packaged foods is best because they pretty much all have sugar hidden in them.

The Eyes Have It.

Your baby is learning right from when it is born. He is learning more from you by watching than you actually need to actively teach him. He is learning by mirroring you and needs eye contact to gain trust.

Studies have shown that babies become very distressed when they are with someone who does not mirror them, or who is preoccupied (like when they are stressed and thinking about work or a problem), or distant. This can also happen in the case of post-natal depression where the mother may not have developed an instant bond or feel inadequate as a parent. It can also happen where parents are told to avoid eye contact with their babies. They are usually told this by others who believe if you give your baby eye contact as you put them to sleep, they will become aroused and that you are giving them a settling tool and they should not rely on you to settle. The babies in these scenarios and studies frantically try to make eye contact, eventually giving up and avoiding eye contact themselves.

Babies and children are exquisitely sensitive, and easily feel confused, frightened or overwhelmed. Parental stress is one of the myriad sources for a baby or child to experience stress. Relax by knowing that it's age appropriate for your baby to rely on you to sleep and that you are teaching your baby to have a calm and connected trusting bond between the two of you by giving them eye contact as you help them to sleep. Avoiding eye contact may mean that confusion and stress accumulates within his body and he can cope with it by using the strategy of turning excessively inward or zoning and spacing out. He is taken away from connection with himself and others, including you. You will have noticed this when you have witnessed a baby who is with a blank stare and sucking on something. Older children may sit gazing and will just not answer your question. Others express it by running around constantly and bumping into things and falling over. All of these behaviours are to cope with the feelings they have inside. This accumulated stress and nervous system overload affect their ability to unwind, sleep, concentrate, learn and contribute.

So, by making eye contact with your child, you are ensuring they are unwinding from the day with ease, helping them to trust you and the world around them, release tension and you may find that you actually enjoy it too. The old saying, 'the eyes have it', holds true when it comes to this.

It's Okay to Laugh

Remember there are no rules. The rules are what you feel your baby wants and is content with. If you are trying to be all serious at bed time and it isn't working, perhaps lighten up, sing a song or joke with them about something they find funny. Tickle them a little or pull funny faces; whatever makes you feel happy. Your baby will feel relaxed seeing you happy and will most likely laugh too. Laughing releases great endorphins for both of you and laughing yourselves to sleep can make for a wonderful ritual. I remember many times when I was rocking my baby boy to sleep and he thought my singing voice for "How much is that doggy in the window?" was hilarious. He would laugh every time I made the barking noise and he literally giggled himself to sleep. He would then go heavy and limp in my arms and I knew he was in a deep sleep before I put him to bed and I would sometimes even hear him giggle in his sleep. It was such a special noise. It would be silent and I'd hear a loud infectious laughter. I thought he would wake himself up but he didn't. It must have been a beautiful dream. If your baby happens to laugh when you are trying to create a 'quiet' sleep ritual; don't say, "Shh" or worry about it. Go with it and laugh too. It may be just what you both need after a massive day.

Patch Adams was famous for healing people with laughter. Imagine what it could do in your sleep?

Sleep Aids

I recently saw a mum who was walking her baby to sleep as it cried. The baby was four-and-a-half-months old and it was clearly upset; hence the crying. Naturally, a mum gets upset if her baby is too. I asked her if she might consider taking her out of the pram for a cuddle and a breastfeed? She said, "No, I don't want to do that because then the baby would rely on it". So here are my thoughts on this: your baby DOES rely on it! You need to ask yourself if you are okay with that. Are you okay with cuddling your baby to sleep? Do you think you would like a cuddle to sleep? I know I like to have a hot shower and maybe even a warm organic oat milk cacao before bed. Sometimes I play music or read to help me fall asleep. What if this baby's tiny stomach, which is the size of its fist needed a top-up because it was growing at a such a rapid rate, that the baby found it hard to go to sleep hungry? I know I do. In fact when I was pregnant, I was so hungry I'd wake in the night to eat a bowl of cereal or fruit in order to be able to go back to sleep. We do it for ourselves and growing baby's health in the womb so why not out of the womb too? When does it stop?

I found it fascinating to learn that when you 'spoon' your partner at night in bed, you both only fall asleep when your breathing and heart beats synchronise. It's typical of the mammalian species. Babies are the same. In fact we are the only mammals that don't keep our young close. Besides the benefits of breastfeeding your baby to sleep for the baby, there are benefits for the mum too. Not only is it age appropriate, but every time you do so, you both get hormones that help you to sleep. Ever heard the saying "sleep while the baby is sleeping?" The release of oxytocin helps you to not have a care in the world but that of your baby's wellbeing. It's the most peaceful feeling if you don't let it be ruined by others' misconceptions about it being wrong to let your baby 'rely' on it. In fact, it's the most natural thing in the world. Our bodies are designed that way and if anything YOU rely on it so that you can continue on in a healthy way.

There can be many sleeping aids and many things that your baby may rely on. Just be patient and go easy on your little person. Your baby may have a favourite toy they like to hold onto. I know if many who hold on to DVD covers of their favourite show or a book- hardly a cuddly toy but go with whatever works. My little boy wants to hold onto a toy pram sometimes. Now that's hardly a teddy bear but it's funny and he is happy. Whatever your sleeping aid — a toy, a rocking motion or story and song — make it enjoyable as you allow your little person to show you who they are and what they like. Contrary to what others may say, a sleeping aid is perfectly healthy.

Temperatures

When your baby was in your womb, he had the temperature all sorted. It was completely regulated by you and your body. It was about 37 degrees Celsius. When your baby comes out of that warm womb, it can be very overwhelming and unsettling to have different temperatures from bath to dressed to undressed for a nappy change to dressed again and then to a warm feed and only to get cold again, and so on and so on. The quickest way for your baby to regulate his temperature is through a breastfeed or being held by you.

Currently, health professionals do not recommend a specific room temperature for a healthy baby's room. However you may like to try and keep the room temperature at around 22- 26 degrees for your baby to sleep in. This might be a good temperature that allows you to still wrap or cover your baby. Never cover your baby's head when putting them to sleep because we expel heat from our head and if your baby is too hot, they can expel the heat and regulate their body temperature through the head. If it is covered, it may overheat them. You can check your baby and their temperature while they sleep by placing your hand gently behind the neck if they are covered everywhere else. When your baby is very young, they do not have the capability to shiver so they rely on you and your touch or breastfeeds to regulate their temperature. Shivering raises the body's core temperature. Of course, the best way to ensure your baby's temperature is just right is by co-sleeping, as you mutually regulate each other's temperature.

Massage

Research shows that touch can affect every aspect of our lives. Nurturing touch, or lack of it, can impact on the way we think, feel and relate to others. When my husband worked as a volunteer paramedic in South Africa some of the babies were taken to a hospital and if they weren't touched after two weeks they failed to thrive. It's just so sad to see a baby neglected of touch and they need a whole bunch of it. In fact the more you touch your baby, the smarter you are helping him to become.

Infant massage is something that a baby can benefit from during all ages and stages and ideally should be massaged from birth through to adolescence. Keep in mind that premature babies may find it too stimulating, but your qualified infant massage instructor can help you prepare your baby for massage with kangaroo care, touch therapy and containment techniques where your baby is brought back to a foetal position. This technique can be one daily which provides stability and predictability for the premature infant.

Infant massage uses gentle, tactile stimulation, and loving verbal communication to deepen the relationship between parents and their baby. It is a shared experience, done with the baby, not to the baby. The strokes used can be both stimulating and relaxing. It is easy to learn and a beautiful experience to have with your baby. The main benefits of infant massage are bonding between mother or carer and baby. This can be extremely helpful for a mother suffering from postnatal depression, or a parent that is struggling to connect with their child. The more skin to skin contact, the more oxytocin is released, and you both feel the love.

Other benefits through the stimulating part of a massage are the positive effects on the various systems. Research shows that the respiratory, muscular, circulatory and immune systems all benefit and can improve. It's a perfect way of becoming aware of your baby's cues and understanding their very unique language. This helps build confidence as a parent.

Another benefit is relief from certain health challenges such as colic and tummy discomfort. There are specific massage techniques that can improve baby's digestion. Other areas of relief are teething, growing pains, chest and sinus build up. The other benefit in a non-stimulating part of a massage is relaxation. Finally, massage can help baby with increased flexibility and healthy sleeping patterns are also promoted when both parents and babies are relaxed.

It's best to be taught how to massage your baby by a qualified infant massage consultant. Classes can be fun and strokes are easy to learn. While intent of touch is powerful, there are certain strokes or times that a baby may find massage overstimulating and unsettling, negating the effects.

Here are some tips and examples:

It's imperative to ask a baby for permission to massage them by placing the palms of your hands above them and asking the question: "Would you like a massage?" Your baby may give you signs that he is not wanting a massage by avoiding eye contact and moving around, crying, fussing or pulling their ears. Performing a permission sequence means you not only respect your baby's feelings and needs but you develop a trust and bond with them. The most important lesson from respecting the permission sequence is that you teach your child how to say "No" when necessary. Children are taught that when they say "Yes" to an adult, they are being good and may say "yes" to please you. Therefore, it is really important to be careful on how you phrase your question. Do not say, "Do you want a massage or not?" Quite simply, "Would you like a massage?", hold hands above and watch for signs. If an adult ever wants to touch your child inappropriately; you have given them the skills to recognise when it is okay to say, "no". There are too many times in a child's life where they are taught to say "yes" to an adult and understand that saying "yes" will please them, so this part of daily massage is a very important part of listening and respecting your child.

There may be medical contraindications and times where you may not massage your child. It could be because of a medical condition and so it would be important to gain approval from your doctor. Local contraindications are times when you can massage but just not in a contraindicated area. This may be, for example, over a cut, bruise or burn or an unhealed navel. Another time they may not wish to have a massage is during about 8-14 months during which they have started crawling and or walking and enjoying their new found independence. However, you can reintroduce and offer massage again after a few months. Continue to offer regularly. The benefits of infant massage are not just for the baby but also for the massager. Through skin-to-skin contact, it can have a real impact on mothers and postnatal depression as oxytocin is released.

Health benefits of infant massage:
- Relaxation of skeletal muscles
- Increases lymphatic and blood circulation
- Reduces anxiety and improves alertness
- Strengthens the immune system — lymphatic exercises and massage
- Improves sleep by increasing serotonin levels and regulates melatonin levels; balancing melatonin secretion rhythms
- Increases weight gain in low birth weight infants
- Reduces crying
- Enhances bonding
- Enhances body awareness

With premature babies, there are different touch therapy techniques which a baby can receive in preparation for massage. A containment technique which doesn't stimulate the infant's reflexes and recreates the sensation of being in the womb can help the baby. This coupled with skin-to-skin care via 'kangaroo care'. Kangaroo care is where the baby experiences skin-to-skin contact with the parent; via an unbuttoned shirt they can place the baby on their chest that helps provide stability and predictability. This eases them into massage that can be done, monitoring your baby's signs and signals.

Infant massage should never be performed when a baby is crying unless it is to help with colic. Colic hasn't any known cause, but here are the telling signs:

- Painful cry that lasts for hours each day
- The baby pulls his legs into his chest
- The cry happens at the same time each day
- The baby will have a distended or bloated abdomen.

There is a special colic sequence that can be performed twice a day for two-four weeks which is when you may start to see improvement. It is very important to be taught though by a trained infant massage instructor on how to do this to your child.

Colic is an umbrella term for the above symptoms and even though the medical profession don't really know what causes it, theories expressed by health professionals on the cause of colic are:

- Lactose or cow's milk protein (casein) intolerance
- Intestinal spasms caused by wind getting trapped in the baby's intestines
- Immaturity of the baby's digestive system
- Incorrect position of the spine
- Foods that the mother is consuming and the baby is also receiving via breast milk like: caffeine, wheat, eggs, fish, nuts, chocolate, alcohol, citrus fruits, spices and carbonated soft drinks.

While infant massage can help with colic, this illustrates the importance of recognising just how delicate the developing digestive system is and why it's important to continue into extended breastfeeding if you can and change you and/or your baby's diet. See the problem as the solution. The benefits of changing your diet for your baby mean that you get to be as healthy as can be too.

Prevention and Witching Hour (Cluster feeding)

This 'problem' time before night can also be seen as the solution. Some have named the hour before bed, the 'witching hour' where babies seem to be very unsettled and may cry out of control or at least behave in an erratic manner. I found this term never entered our household because I used the term 'prevention is better than cure' and would always continue to be aware of my baby's tired signs BEFORE it got to the stage that they had to get unsettled. It's only natural for you to feel upset if you are really tired. If you have had a massive day or a stressful day and know you're tired but still stay awake and try and watch television or something like that, you will land up being a little grumpy yourself. Try to imagine what it must be like for your baby and create a ritual — not a routine, but a nice pattern where the hour or two before bed is a relaxing unwinding of a very big day.

Turn this challenging time into a time of gratitude where your baby is really asking that you have some unwinding time with him. If you are not working or working part time, the most ideal scenario is to try and be home by around 4pm so you can relax while preparing dinner and create some calm in your home without rushing around, and feeling stressed and unorganised. Turn off the television and radio because at the time before your baby's bed time there will be news airing and these images and tones are hardly relaxing for either you or the baby.

Rather than call this time 'witching hour', try to call it your 'peace hour' and 'unwind time' and see it as reconnecting and nourishing as you release tension of a day and prepare for the next. Sometimes no matter how relaxing you create your space and time, you and your baby may still feel upset and may protest a little. It needn't be an actual cry as such but a whine as your baby releases some of the built-up tension from the day. Just keep loving, empathetic and holding your child with an understanding tone and they will eventually fall asleep, feeling safe in your arms as they felt emotionally supported by you.

If you are breastfeeding, your 'witching hour' may be as a result of 'cluster feeding' time. It may also actually occur with bottle fed babies too. Cluster feeding is what it sounds like: A group of breast or bottle feedings closely spaced together; usually baby-initiated.

Generally babies will cluster feed in the evenings, though some like to cluster feed in the wee hours of the morning, just like what the animal kingdom do as they graze before sunset and then sleep, only to wake in the early hours of the morning to graze until sunrise again. This feeding pattern can be very different from what the baby does during the day—just when mum and dad would like to start unwinding, baby seems to gear up and want to feed more often. So you could call this hour the 'fussy' hour. It is where parents and mothers usually jump to the conclusion that they are not making enough milk for their baby. Why else would the baby keep coming back to the breast? But remember: Being at the breast provides nutrition for the baby, but it also provides comfort. Suckling is a reflex and can help a cranky baby calm down, so cluster feeding is often a baby's way of trying to soothe and regulate himself and not just fill up for the long hours that lie ahead that feel like a fast because they are sleeping and not feeding. The great news is that it is typically right after a cluster feed that your baby will have his longest stretch of sleep within a 24-hour period. This is where you will get your best sleep too, so save all the chores you have to do for when baby is happy and alert and playing and use this time to sleep.

Follow the Leader – Baby must first be tired

Who's the leader? My Dad asked me once: "Oh who's in control?" The truth is it's the baby. If you want to control or train something, get a puppy. While you are your baby's 'leader' and your baby is learning more from you, you can actually be led by your baby too. When you follow your baby's lead and cues, you will find it rather easy to settle them without tears because they are ready to be settled. Your baby will give you signs that they are getting tired or restless and rather than watching the time, you are watching your baby. Once your baby is really tired, you can start your settling ritual. So follow your baby's lead. There's no point looking at the clock and thinking he must be asleep by a certain time every night. Day to day events change and so does your baby's 'routine' or moods depending on what has happened within a 24-hour period.

It can take twice as long and become more frustrating for both parties if you follow a strict 'routine' and try to put your baby to sleep when they are not tired.

To get to know when your baby will most likely be ready for a sleep, there are a certain amount of hours that a baby can handle as 'awake' time.

Go With The Flow

The key to happiness for both mother and baby is to not make any plans and not get caught up in a 'routine'. Rituals are very important and provide cues for your baby to feel comfortable with knowing what is going to happen next. However a strict routine can leave mother feeling confused or frustrated when she finds out her baby isn't into it. Many have suggested that there be a routine of "Eat. Play. Sleep." This may sound like a good plan at first, but if you think about it, it limits you and your baby on when you can do what. It doesn't allow for flexibility and doesn't consider what may be going on that day: too hot, more tired, change in seasons, a growth spurt, a development growth spurt and other sorts of milestones. It would be like telling you when you should eat and work. For example, only letting your baby have milk when it wakes may be very unsettling for them. Babies like to suck and it is natural for them to want milk to fall asleep to. It's age appropriate. If you are breast feeding then all the more reason. Don't make too many plans.

Sleep When Baby Sleeps

This is so cliché', such an overused phrase and a common tip parents love to share. So much so, that I didn't listen. I remember being on Facebook one night at 10pm, downloading photos to show off to every one of my newborn and a friend wrote to me: "What are you, mad? Sleep while the baby sleeps." I was running high on hormones that made me feel in top of the world and I was fine but then I crashed. It really hit me hard when I did too much instead of recovering and literally sleeping when the baby sleeps. Okay, so why then? Why not just when someone's playing with the baby and perhaps you go and have a day nap? Because you are so synchronised that if you follow your baby's sleep pattern, you will actually get the right amount and type of sleep. It also helps to know that when your baby is sleeping, you naturally feel settled and relaxed. I would sometimes get really grumpy and irritable and then my baby may have fallen asleep and all of a sudden I was too. This especially happened on trips in the car. I'd wake after 40 minutes or so and it felt like I was on earth again.

Lovely Lavender Feet

Did you know that the largest organ in your body is the skin? In fact your skin is a carrier, not a barrier with many orifices called pores. Your pores can absorb anything and everything. From good oils to carcinogens found in some personal hygiene products we should avoid like SLS (sodium lauryl sulphate), the foaming ingredient in soaps. Good oils absorbed into the feet can be really relaxing for your baby, especially during the times of learning to walk. Dilute a couple of drops of pure essential lavender oil into some warm water and make a foot bath for baby. Or, put a few drops into some pure cold-pressed coconut oil and give your baby a foot massage just before sleep time. Starting massage with the legs best way to begin a massage and is highly recommended because it is the least invasive area of the body. Lavender has been known to have relaxing properties and has been used by aromatherapists for many years.

Story Time Rituals

As you are undressing your baby, putting on pyjamas, changing the nappy at the end of the day or giving a baby massage, you may like to slowly talk through the events of the day that you and your baby shared. Just like you and your partner may like to unwind by chatting over a hot drink and telling the tales of the things you did, so too does your baby. It can be a sort of offloading for some or reminiscing for others. Begin this from day dot. Even though you think your baby cannot understand you, he's certainly learning and also enjoying the sound of your voice. You will notice that your baby may get excited by the stories you tell or it may calm and sooth them. It's also a great interactive distraction for when they get a bit older as toddlers and find it very boring to just lie there and have their nappy changed. It can be very unsettling for them to be still for long periods of time so this sort of storytelling can be something they really look forward to. There may even be a favourite toy that they may like to hold as you tell them. The toy may be something they played with or learned something new about. Make your voice sound animated and enjoy the reminiscing of the day you had with them too.

You may have a favourite story book you read to your baby before sleep. If it is the same book every time, you get them used to a healthy bedtime ritual.

Cluster Feeding – Feeder is Queen

Your new baby may want to sleep quite a bit after your birth and mamas usually wait anxiously near their babies in the hope that they'll wake soon and relieve them of their breast milk they have been making. In the beginning, it's common for the feeder to have an oversupply until your baby controls the amount it requires and you experience less engorgement. However, in the next four-six weeks, you can expect to feed around every two hours. This means from the time the feed starts, then two hours after that. Sometimes it is more often and supply is being established. Every baby and mother is so unique and different. Every situation is one of a kind. Babies like to feed really often and sometimes constantly at least one time within a 24-hour period. This is usually just before they first go to sleep at night. They may feed non-stop, swapping sides for hours which is called a 'cluster feed' as though they're storing up for the big night ahead, constantly grazing just like in the animal kingdom before dusk. It is after the cluster feed that the baby will then have their biggest or rather, longest sleep of that 24 hour period. This is when mama MUST go to sleep too because this is the best quality and quantity sleep you will get. It may be difficult adjusting to this as a new mother especially because this time could be right at your one on one time you normally had with your partner. However, even if you do this only three nights a week, it will make a huge difference to how you cope and your overall moods and wellbeing. You can always make your one on one time with your partner at another time of the day. After all, it's only for a short time while baby is small and this time will pass quickly. Try to make your partner be more involved with this cluster feeding time and help by getting you water to drink. As you swallow a sip of water, relax your shoulders and allow your milk to 'let down' and exhale. It's a great time to unwind at the end of the day and bond as a new family.

The New Wrap

Wrapping your baby to help it to sleep has been around in Western Cultures for many years. It comes from a place of

Wanting your baby to have the feeling that he is still in the womb, tight and secure

Minimising startle reflexes when they are small that may wake them. Their arms and hands can move in jerky motions as they fall into different phases of sleep and may sometimes hit themselves in the face. They may not even be aware that what hit them is their own hand so it can startle and wake them. Wrapping their arms down stops this.

However, other cultures have never believed in wrapping at all. There are new thoughts, and here's the 'middle ground' again, on now wrapping he baby for the secure feeling but leaving the arms out. You'll notice some babies like to sleep with their arms above their head. You can see a whole range of different type of wraps and sleeping bag style zip-up wraps that allow arms to be in that exact position. Try different ways and see which works for you and your baby. You may like to even wrap the arms but do it loosely. Some babies actually do like to be wrapped very tightly. Just monitor when your baby may be starting to get more active and aware and prefer not to be wrapped anymore. This could be anywhere from 3-10 months old. Once again, everyone is so different. To wrap or not to wrap is the question.

Co-Sleeping

The best way to really get some quality sleep, believe it or not, is by trying a form of co-sleeping. There are many types of definitions and arrangements. There is no one size fits all for everyone but at some stage of yours and your baby's life, you will find yourself naturally wanting to share the bed, even if it is because your toddler woke because of a nightmare and wants a cuddle to help fall back to sleep.

You may like to have your baby in bed with you, or you may decide to be on a mattress on the floor. The baby could be in a bassinet between you. Another form of co-sleeping is where the baby is not in the bed, but in your room, in a side cart off your bed, or in a hammock or cot in your room. The co-sleeping rule of thumb is for the baby to be within arm's reach.

Despite what some say, co-sleeping is not dangerous unless you are not careful and/or under the influence of drugs/medications/alcohol that stop your body's natural response system. A mother will always hear her baby "Aah" before anything could possibly happen to the child. In fact, on the contrary, you are within arm's reach, just like other mammalian species and can attend to your baby's needs should something happen.

One night our baby had woken repeatedly every 20 minutes and by 1am we were both so exhausted from attending to him, and were trying to rock him back to sleep. He started convulsing and vomiting. This happened without cries and he brought up some fish and peach that he ate that night. Perhaps the fish was not fresh or had a particularly high level of mercury. Perhaps his body intelligently rejected the toxic food? Whatever the reason, he felt much better after the expulsion and slept much better too. We shuddered to think what may have happened if he was not in our room.

> **How to Sleep your Baby Safely:**
> 1. Sleep baby on the back from birth, not on the tummy or side
> 2. Sleep baby with face uncovered (no doonas, pillows, lambs wool, bumpers or soft toys)
> 3. Avoid exposing babies to tobacco smoke before birth and after
> 4. Provide a safe sleeping environment (safe cot, safe mattress, safe bedding)
> 5. Sleep baby in their own safe sleeping environment next to the parent's bed for the first six to twelve months of life

For safe co-sleeping tips, go to www.sidsandkids.com.au

Since its inception in the early 1990s, the campaign has reduced the incidence of SIDS by 85% saving over 6000 babies lives. Vigilance is still required in delivering our Safe Sleeping message to the broad community as sadly the cause of sudden infant death syndrome remains unknown with more research into the cause still needed.

You can reduce waking up to check that mum is here by co-sleeping. Since you put your baby to bed a few hours ahead of yourself he may become anxious, needing to check that you are near. If he wakes up and you are not there, he will no doubt cry to get your attention. He may sleep less deeply, with an alertness to your presence and waking up more often, even when you are right next to her. He has no way of knowing for sure that you will be there. The baby can only feel safe to sleep deeply when she has no doubt that you are always with her. Therefore, co-sleeping is best when practised full-time.

However, your baby will still be able to adjust and get deeper sleep eventually. The challenge in our Western world lives is to figure out how to co-sleep and still have some sort of 'life' with our partners. You are not alone. Many responsive and attached parents put their baby to bed ahead of themselves so they can connect with their spouses or nurture themselves. Although the couple's connection is important, the evening is the worst time for it because it is the time a baby needs you the most. Be creative in finding time for you and your spouse, and learn to connect with each other with baby in arms. Your connection time may be in the day or lunch break. Life is now different but bringing you both more joy and only this stage will last a little while. It is just a stage.

You may like to try putting your baby to sleep but be prepared that when he wakes, that you may need to transfer him with you so that you at least get an hour or two alone before the togetherness you will share that night.

Rules to make co-sleeping easier

- Go to bed at the same time as your baby or move her bedtime gradually to match yours. This way you get more sleep and your baby will learn to trust that you are always next to him and gradually diminish the need for check-up wakeups'. After a while, when she is sure you are always with him, she will wake up without crying and only as much as she needs to breastfeed.

- Alternately, you can let your baby fall asleep in your arms while you are still up with your husband or with your other children.

- When your baby naps, try to sleep with him for at least one day sleep or at least put him down right next to you so if he shows the slightest motion you can promptly touch him, cuddle or breastfeed again to establish security.

- Stay sleepy when you offer the breast at night so you are never really waking. You'll need to wear easy to remove clothing or no top at all. Stay in the dark and have a glass of water nearby. Minimising motion and change will help both of you to go back to sleep. You can even fall asleep or doze while breastfeeding.

- If you need to change a wet nappy, have it handy and change it under the blanket laying down.

- Remove all lighting that may arouse the part of the brain from a deep sleep like mobile phones and lamps or television and alarm clocks.

- Try not to count the number of times your baby wakes up, what time it is or how many feeds you have done. It may cause stress and tiredness. Be at peace with the process.

- Each time your baby wakes up, remember how much your baby loves you and how you enjoy the feeling of his soft skin.

I remember when I couldn't go back to sleep after resettling. I stopped looking at the clock and started looking forward to another wake where I could have the chance to have a cuddle again. I would sometimes look at his angel face in the slight moon light and wonder about the miracle that he is. I felt much more refreshed in the morning and had more energy for the day in these times.

Tag Team Sleeps

Whichever way you choose to sleep, near or away from your baby, being responsive is 24-7. It's full time and is hard. It's not meant to be easy every day. You will have days where you just didn't get very good sleep, no matter what you tried. It's just a part of being a new mum, it is just a phase and the investment does pay off.

In these trying times, a really creative way of getting sleep if you have a partner (single parenting is even harder and I have full admiration for the job you do on your own), is to tag team. For example, one parent may be up to settle and if your baby protests then he may be hungry and need a feed, but if he does not protest, you may find that you can get some sleep while it is your partner that does the first settles. Then while it is your turn, after a few hours, your partner can then get some sleep. Swapping means you are a team and it takes a team to raise this healthy child. Your partner may need to work and choose to sleep in a separate room. Though please note, that fathers rarely ever wake when co-sleeping is practised and breastfeeding mothers can attend to the baby very quickly before any crying happens.

Another 'tag team' idea is to have the mother be up with the baby all night and let the father sleep. Then he wakes early to let her sleep from say 6am-8am. The father may be getting the other children ready for school and looking after the baby while you get some quality two hours. If the father has to go to work early in the morning as my husband did most days, we would arrange that he would come home in the lunch break if possible to give me a sleep then if I hadn't already slept with our baby in the day when he was sleeping too.

Have a think about your schedules and where you may be able to tag team some sleep. Whenever I see a dad walking with a pram and a baby, I often wonder and hope that Mother is getting some really good 'shut eye'.

Chapter Eight

Empowering You

Dealing with Unwanted Criticism or Lack Of Supportive Comments

"You look tired." "Are you sure you're coping?" "How come the house is always so messy?" "Can't you clean it while he sleeps?" "Ohh, so your baby isn't sleeping through the night yet…" These are some of the criticisms directed at new mothers from others in our Western world. They are criticisms that can leave postpartum mums with feelings of inadequacy and depression, suggesting she is failing as a responsible parent. When the subject of sleep arises, instead of support, it is criticism offered or "my way worked best". Remember that it's unnatural to have everything 'all together' if you want to parent in a gentle and natural way, enjoying your baby and allowing yourself to heal and make a transition as a new mother, easier.

It's really tough trying to gain confidence and certainty being the mother you want to be for your child when other people's opinions get in the way. Most often, unwanted criticism will come at a time when you are extremely tired and you already have hormones flying around that make you extra emotional. It usually happens to first-time mothers and by the time you have your next child, people do tend to back off and give you space. It's because by then, not only do they presume you know what you are doing, but you actually do know what you are doing. When someone suggests something they think will help you, it's important to listen and then thank them for their concern. After all, they really do want to help you and are doing so the only way they know how. It's the way they were parented or parent. Everyone does things so differently but you may take what they say with a grain of salt and adapt it to suit you one day or you may find it really unhelpful and perhaps even hurtful.

Please don't ever take the criticism personally and maintain your confidence no matter how tired or hormonal you feel. Most of the time the suggestions are coming from their own personal experience. It may have worked for their child and that family, but it also makes the parent feel better about themselves if they prove their advice to be the best. Sometimes a mother can feel confused or challenged if she sees something you did that she wished she had the support or courage to do. It's their 'stuff', not yours.

The best way to handle these situations, especially if you care about that person, is to quote from a research article or knowledgeable person like your midwife or lactation specialist.

The Australian Breastfeeding Association suggests that by quoting someone else like this means that nobody's feelings get hurt.

You can reply, "Thanks so much for that. I can see how much you care, but our lactation specialist suggested that we …blah, blah, blah." Or, "The research we've read about that, suggests … etc."

Below are some common questions and comments and examples of how to respond and deal with them.

Does your baby 'sleep through' now? Or …Why isn't he getting enough sleep?

My baby's getting just the right amount of sleep he needs. We are not actually designed to sleep all through the night as babies only have two stages of sleep unlike an adult that has three. There are many healthy reasons that they need to wake for nervous system development. For example just to rock them helps them to develop the vestibular part of the brain.

(If your baby does four-five hours in a row, this is good sleep) Yes, he's doing wonderfully. (Every baby wakes at least once or twice for a refill and most mums don't always tell you if theirs does.)

How come your baby's not 'sleeping through' yet?

Research shows his brain is only fully developed at around five years of age and won't have adult sleep patterns yet.

We are so happy to follow our baby's lead and wake to resettle if he wants to wake. We like to trust his instincts and do things naturally. Thank you for your concern though; it is tough sometimes but we feel the investment is already paying off as he is a confident and emotionally secure child.

Why does your baby feed all night?

Because breast milk isn't just food and some babies use it to catch up on immunity or analgesic properties for teething. It's natural for a breastfed baby and very common to feed several times during the night as the quality of milk a mother makes is better as she produces prolactin which puts baby into a deeper sleep and helps mum sleep too.

Also, his stomach is only the size of a marble and needs to refill often as he is growing at a rapid rate. But you needn't worry as you cannot overfeed a breastfed baby. They control exactly what type of calories they need with each feed.

You're not letting your baby exercise their lungs by crying

There's no research to actually support this statement. Adults certainly don't exercise their lungs by crying. Crying causes an adrenal cascade to occur including the release of cortisol, commonly called a flight or fight response. Why would I want to stress my baby and flood his body with stress chemicals for no reason?

You're going to spoil your child and they'll become a spoilt brat if you attend to them every time they cry.

Research shows it's the exact opposite. By attending to my child's cries for help, I'm helping him to feel secure in his attachment to me, because his brain is still developing. Eventually, when he is old enough, he will have a brain that's developed enough to understand how to deal with stress better. I feel happy knowing that I'm helping him to cope with his feelings more. They are valid feelings too.

Why are you still breastfeeding after 12 months? Hasn't he got teeth?

While there are a myriad of things you could reply with, like "It's completely natural to give my baby my milk," or "I'm sorry you can't see the beauty in it. It's a personal choice." The best way to address this one is to refer to research and say things like. "The World Health Organization says that you should breastfeed until around the age of two to four." Another good fact is that, "Lactation specialists say that after the age of 12 months, the antibodies in my milk double." This helps people to understand that breastfeeding is not just food and the enormous necessary immunity they need from extended breastfeeding, not to mention attachment issues and how unique every case is, especially in other cultures that do not question extended breastfeeding.

Looking After Number Two- You

Healthy You, Healthy Baby

Because baby's needs come first, it's very normal that you'll forget about looking after yourself. In fact sometimes you may even find that you don't feel like painting your nails, let alone washing your hair like you used to, but you just don't care when your new bundle of joy gives you a smile or giggles sweetly. Other days, you may crave having the time where you used to do that. On these days, it's important to plan an hour or two where you can do something for yourself now and then. At first, you may not want to, but as time gets on, it's okay to feel like you want to start looking after you too. There's something called 'mother's guilt' where apparently a mother always feels like she should be doing something for her children before she does anything for herself. It's only natural to want the best for your child and put their needs first; and rightly so.

On the other hand, people just love helping babies. The best way to really help a baby is to help the baby's mother.

The only way to look after you is to have someone else look after you.

You see, most of the time what the mother needs is to be looked after exactly the same way the baby needs to be looked after. A mother needs to be mothered too. When you claim your role as a new mother, you also need to be mothered so you can feel like one for your divine baby.

- On any day, dress your baby up in your favorite clothes and take him out to the corner store to chat to the neighbors and try to make yourself feel lovely too because then people naturally will comment about how gorgeous your baby is and this will make you feel proud and more in love as you talk about him. It will give you the energy to carry on, even when you thought you had none left. As tired as I was, I made one rule — to put on a mineral foundation make-up (I had a natural one from clay I loved), which covered the dark circles under my eyes. I did this while baby was watching a Baby Einstein DVD, or I'd interact with him and include him in what I was doing. But the point is, it made me feel like I could start the day and face the world. On days where I didn't wear make-up, it would remind me of how tired I was and only made things harder. Other days, I just accepted that I was tired and wasn't meant to always feel or look amazing and was just kinder to myself by lowering my expectations.

- Enjoy your baby. At the end of the day, you aren't going to be able to 'achieve' as many things as you used to before you were pregnant. I have put the word in inverted commas because us Western women do too much. We work too hard and we rarely take the time to smell the roses. Life can often rush us by and before you know it, you're asking where the years have gone. Try to see something that goes 'wrong' like your baby falling asleep at a particular time, a chance for you to have one too. Or if your baby won't let you put him down, actually enjoy the touch of his skin and the smell and enjoy that moment. It's a forced meditation for you and an 'emotional refuelling' or 'check – in' for them. You probably need it as much as your baby does but you just don't realise it.

- If you find you cannot sleep during the day when your baby does then make a promise that you will at least lie down and relax or meditate or just be still and read. This starts to prepare the mind to unwind and your body will eventually follow.

Separation, Distress, and Dealing with it

Separation and distress can occur during or after a traumatic birth or an emotional break-up in the family. It can be one of the hardest things a mother has to deal with.

Most of us don't realise that no matter how stressful our birth was or the scenario, it's best to try and keep our babies close.

Search for the support you need around you that helps you to do so.

Keeping your baby away from you can create challenges with breast milk hormones and general wellbeing.

Many mothers experience mastitis as a result of expressing milk too early and this can interfere with the supply-demand rule. It can be confused for the flu because of its flu-like symptoms. Please remember to consult a good lactation consultant or a breastfeeding counsellor from the ABA. You may have challenges at first with nipples, feeding and other breastfeeding issues but there is always a way to get the right help and overcome it all naturally.

Postnatal depression is the most prevalent mood disorder and western world illness associated with child birth. The condition is characterised by irritability, anger, low energy levels and feelings of guilt. Please don't be quick to label yourself and give yourself time to heal. Some of your feelings may be a natural response to a stressful situation. Don't feel ashamed to seek help.

A study was done on massaging infants and infant massage has been known to play a significant role in helping PND. Forty full-term one-three year-olds born to depressed adolescent mothers were randomly assigned to a set amount of massage and rocking time, twice a week for six weeks. After this period the massaged infants showed significant weight gain, improvement in sociability and soothability as well as biochemical stress levels.

In summary, the need for touch for both parent and child is great and plays a huge role in how a parent can thrive. Sometimes the worst thing that can happen is that the baby will be taken away from the mother as some health professionals think that it's important for the two to be apart from each other so that the mother can get some sleep. However, taking the baby away from the mother may be risking milk supply issues and both parties are missing out on the love hormone oxytocin which is imperative for wellbeing. With touch, this powerful hormone is released and massage is a great way to ensure this happens.

Baby monkeys grew up anxious and anti-social after the stress of separation from their mothers, a study says. It suggests changes to the brains of infant monkeys may be irreversible, and the study could be a model for humans. An early shock to the system may leave the monkeys prone to a life of anxiety, poor social skills and depression.

But the work could point the way to better management and treatment of those who live with a legacy of "early adversity".

The report, published in the journal *Proceedings of the National Academy of Sciences*, showed that rhesus monkey babies do not fully recover from the stress of being separated from their mothers at birth.

Some baby monkeys had to be cared for separately if they were at risk from an inexperienced mother, the mother lacked breast milk or the baby would not survive in rainy, cold weather. But even after three years of living a normal social life following the separation, levels of the stress-coping hormone cortisol in these monkeys remained significantly reduced and their bodies' response to stressful events was slower. In monkeys and humans, cortisol is released in stressful situations to mobilise energy stores and aid survival.

Changes to a Developing Brain

But sustained stress and prolonged release of cortisol can lead to severe impairment of some brain regions as they develop.

The baby monkeys that suffered the stress of separation from their mothers went on to be more anxious and less sociable than monkeys that were raised by their mothers.

This study is unique in demonstrating that, for monkeys, the negative effects of separation in infancy cannot be reversed by a later normal social life, write the authors.

These findings may help explain work reported earlier this week in the *American Journal of Psychiatry* (AJP) on the link between childhood maltreatment and later depression in humans.

Both of these studies suggest that stress on infants has long-term negative effects.

Dr Andrea Danese of King's College London, co-author of AJP study, said:

> "In this case you have findings in animals that resemble to an extent the findings in humans both from a behavioural point of view and from a biological point of view."
>
> "If you take studies in humans who have experienced loss I think the findings are quite consistent. Children who lose parents or are separated from parents tend to show more anxious behaviour, and tend also to have changes in the same type of hormones that were measured. In some cases they have poorer social skills, they have more aggressive behaviour."

Long-Term Illnesses

In humans, there also appear to be links between childhood adversity, physiology and other illnesses later in life, possibly through the stress-sensitive immune system.

Dr Danese told BBC News: "Both cortisol and the immune system are related. Cortisol is a very potent anti-inflammatory compound: low cortisol means high inflammation."

"Adults with a history of childhood maltreatment have these elevated inflammation levels. Inflammation is one of the key factors that contribute to a number of age-related conditions like cardiovascular disease, type-2 diabetes and dementia."

"There is something in these stress sensitive systems that is very finely regulated and tuned in childhood. This is because all these systems are developing and maturing during early life."

It appears that stress in childhood, for monkeys and humans, can lead to behavioural and health problems that can only be partially repaired in later life. But there is a positive side to these results.

"The message sounds very negative and I understand why, but from the research point of view I think it is positive because it points to the problem and once we understand the causes of all these behavioural problems, we can then start trying to find the potential cures," said Dr Danese.

He added: "In humans, there is a movement in psychiatry to be moved earlier in life. More and more we're trying to work with young people who have been exposed to traumatic experiences, to maltreatment, to try to see how we can help them overcome their depressive symptoms or work with families and try to avoid the recurrence of the traumatic event."[1]

---

1 http://www.bbc.co.uk/news/science-environment-14562120

In circumstances such as an emergency c-section or separation from mother and baby that is out of your control, there are other ways of making sure you can connect and bond to ensure a healthy start to life and increase chances of lactation.

Losing post baby weight

Every mother's battle with losing weight post pregnancy has been a heartfelt one. Each mother's dedication to her child may result in putting themselves second. Reaching for a quick and easy meal so that sleep can take a priority may not be the best option and who has time to exercise? Looking after you will not only make you feel better physically but emotionally too. But, it doesn't have to be hard.

By understanding what a baby needs to feel secure and safe emotionally and being committed to providing this, the bonus is that your weight will just fall off! You will find yourself burning calories by pushing the pram, wearing your baby and rocking them to sleep. These are simple things that can be done daily that will help you increase your metabolism and keep your body moving naturally.

Here are my top tips for keeping in shape after baby:

- Breastfeeding and extended breastfeeding is a natural way of making sure you get back to what you were before baby came. Around 1000 extra calories a day are expended through providing milk for your child. Your uterus will contract with each feed right after birth and by breastfeeding beyond 12 months ensures that ever so gradually, you and your baby are getting used to your new appetites. If you wean suddenly, your breasts may lose their size and weaning naturally and gradually can help them remain in the same shape.
- Use movement to help your baby sleep. Not only is this beneficial to your baby's developing brain, but it will also mean that you expend calories by moving your body around rocking them to sleep or bouncing them to sleep on a fit ball.
- Wear your baby. This practice of baby wearing is great for a baby's self-esteem and sleep, but it's also another natural way of losing weight as you have a little extra weight to carry around.
- Incidental exercise. On the days where your baby just wants to be held all the time, think about the benefits to you and your exercise as you may need to hold them in one arm and do the housework with the other. If you need to pick something up, do a squat and use it as an opportunity to stretch or exercise.

- Try to only eat really healthy foods. By eating a really healthy diet, especially if you are breastfeeding, you're ensuring better milk and both of you benefit.
- Try to engage in shorter bursts of exercise but daily. Okay, so you aren't able to head off to the gym for an hour and a half like you used to or at least like you think you should, but just 10 minutes a day of cross training type, weight-bearing exercise is all you need to make a difference. The best piece of gym equipment for this is a vibration machine. Cardio Tech supply these exercise equipment items and the vibrations means doing your squats on them for just ten minutes is equivalent to one hour of exercise as your muscles contract at a rapid rate. The only thing is – you cannot use a vibration machine while pregnant.
- Drink lots of water and graze. Don't skip meals and eat very small meals often. Include protein in every meal for muscle building. It may be boiled eggs, goat's cheese, almonds or chick peas.

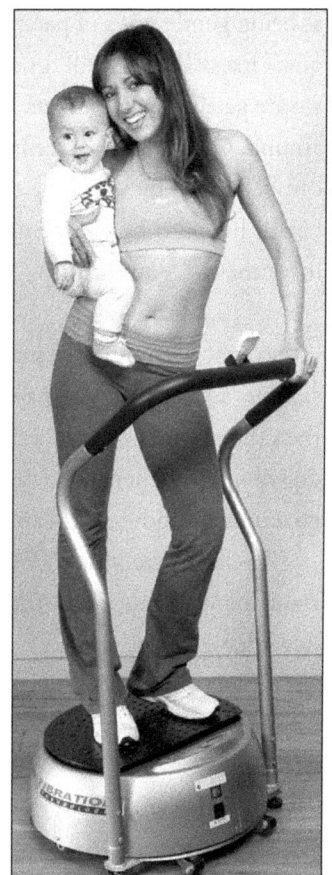

Where's the Support?

If all we all want is the big 's' word – sleep, then the only reason why sleep training techniques that go against our brain's design exist is because there's a market. But parents aren't always aware that there are:

- Other ways, without resorting to these methods
- It's not meant to be easy, but that's okay and there isn't a 'problem' always.
- You CAN find support

If there's no pathological problem and your babies spine and nervous system has been checked by a chiropractor, then your baby may just be healthy and wakeful.

You may have found that everywhere you look, you are being bombarded with stories supporting the CIO and CC methods, even if they are disguised and packaged as being gentle ways of parenting. The sad truth is that just like health care, we expect quick fixes. There's a pill for every ill and we need to be well fast so we can carry on. But we are getting sicker and sicker even though we have the best health care and doctors around. Our lifestyles have become too fast and detached or unnatural. A man's health can be judged by which he takes two at a time, pills or stairs. We have forgotten that health happens by choice not by chance and it's the choices we make today — the investment, in our health — that will help us have a better quality of life tomorrow.

So too, with our investment in our babies, if we can find a way to get the right support and continue to parent in a way that is respectful and feels right in our hearts, then the rewards will pay off in the future. But really, where's the support then? How do we find it? There are actually parenting groups, books and professionals as well as government bodies that can help you and your family.

This list of recommended reads and groups may lead to something else that seems right for you, but know that you can get sleep and support without tears and you never have to feel alone.

Love and respect,

Andi Lew

Helping Hands

Books
- Helping Your Baby to Sleep – Anni Gethin and Beth MacGregor
- The Science of Parenting – Margot Sunderland
- The Womanly Art of Breastfeeding – La Leche International
- Gentle Birth, Gentle Mothering – Dr Sarah Buckley
- Sleeping Like a Baby – Pinky McKay
- Parenting By Heart – Pinky McKay
- And any book or workshop by Pinky McKay
- Breastfeeding Naturally – Jill Day
- Pathways magazine - http://pathwaystofamilywellness.org/
- 8 Infant Sleep Facts Every Parent Should Know – William Sears

Websites:
- www.pinkymckay.com.au
- www.mothersdirect.com.au
- www.breastfeeding.asn.au
- www.incultureparent.com
- www.naturalparenting.com.au
- www.askdrsears.com
- www.midwivesandmothers.com.au
- www.calmbirth.com.au
- www.birthright.com.au

Parenting Groups
- Australian Breastfeeding Association - Your local support group Phone: 1800 mum to mum
- Maternal and Child Health Centres – Your local mother's group
- Attachment Parenting Support Groups http://www.attachmentparentingaustralia.com/support.htm